"Tens of thousands who were without Christ,
having no hope,
caught in the dilemma of a chaotic and polluted
  world,
and no way out,
many of whom sought to escape into drugs
only to find themselves trapped,
have now found the love and beauty of the Christ-
  filled life."

Chuck Smith

The Reproducers
New Life for Thousands

Chuck Smith
with Hugh Steven

A Division of G/L Publications
Glendale, California, U.S.A.

Published by
Regal Books Division, G/L Publications
Glendale, California 91209

Library of Congress Catalog Card No. 72-77115
ISBN 0-8307-0159-1

Fifty percent of all royalties received from
the sale of this book will be used for the
ongoing ministry and outreach of Calvary Chapel.

DEDICATED—

To Jesus
that He may be honored
in all that is written
in this book

Contents

Prologue

There is nothing unique about our area, people are the same all over the world. What God has done here He desires and will do elsewhere. With keen insight and prayerful analysis, Hugh Steven has searched into the records in order to discover the keys the Spirit used to foster this tremendous revival. We have wept and praised together as we have recounted God's marvelous works.

Hugh's recording of these works has been very accurate and, like the work itself, with all naturalness. Within the pages of this manuscript lie the keys for the careful observers, which if they will use, they can also discover the joy of the mighty flow of God's Spirit to a needy world.

Pastor Charles (Chuck) Smith

Chuck

Author's Preface

Jesus began His public ministry in His boyhood home of Nazareth. Luke records the dramatic moment:

> "The Spirit of the Lord is upon me;
> he has appointed me to preach Good News
> to the poor;
> he has sent me to announce that captives
> shall be released and the blind shall see,
> that the downtrodden shall be freed from
> their oppressors,
> and that God is ready to give blessings to all
> who come to him."
>
> Luke 4:18,19 *(LNT)*

Luke tells us that for a long moment everyone looked at Him in amazement.

In recent years many established churchmen have looked with the same amazement at the so-called Jesus Movement. And with equal perplexity at its commune, coffee house and home Bible study ministries. Part of the perplexity is dress. Why the long hair, no shoes or sloppy jeans? There are as many answers to this as there are people in Calvary Chapel. But a more basic question is why success?

"I preach the same basic message as Chuck Smith," said a pastor recently. "But out of a morning congregation of over one thousand, our church has seventy-five to one hundred in the evening service."

Services at Calvary on any given night run fifteen hundred to two thousand and the numbers are growing!

This book is not a treatise on how to have a Jesus Movement. It is an open-ended sharing of what God has done and is doing through Calvary Chapel. For those who can't believe and need a firm explanation, I offer a careful study of Luke 4:18,19 as a key. And I give you the statement of a girl who said, "People come to Calvary because they aren't getting religion or church. They're getting Jesus, His Word and love!"

Appreciation

As a career missionary I am especially responsive to those engaged in cross cultural ministries. In ways similar to an overseas missionary, Chuck Smith has given himself to a unique non-judgmental ministry. For this, his personal warmth and willingness to share his time in long interviews, I thank him.

And I say thank you to Dempster Evans for his refreshing insights and anecdotal material;

to Susan Cato for her willingness to interview, handle recording equipment and extra cameras during a baptism at Corona del Mar;

to each person who took time to share what he sees God doing at Calvary Chapel;

to my wife, Norma, for her love, unselfish encouragement and skill as my efficient collaborator, typist and editor;

to all who release those held captive to self and open spiritually blinded eyes by sharing the Good News of God's love in Jesus Christ;

and special gratitude and great praise to God for Jesus Christ and for His help and work of grace in allowing me to write this book.

Hugh

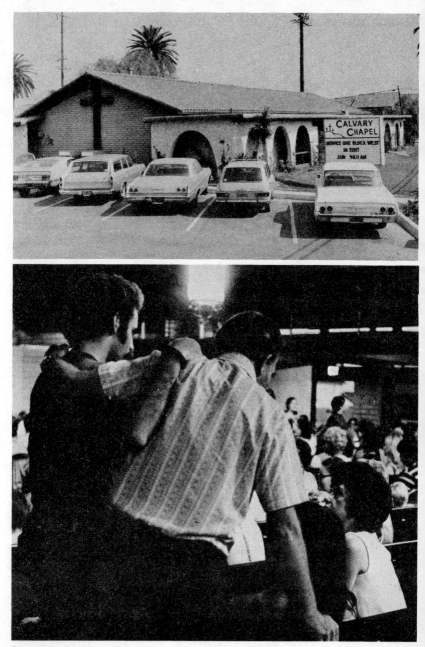

People hungry for the truth of Jesus Christ crowded out the new Calvary sanctuary. As the sign indicates, a tent now accommodates the growing fellowship.

CHAPTER ONE

Hang the Eulogy

It is a Sunday late in the afternoon. The day, alive and brilliant, has been swept clean of all smog by the sea breeze from nearby Costa Mesa. The sun balances on the horizon like a big red balloon. This is southern California in all its glory!

Warm sun, blue sky and sea breezes are not all that make southern California glorious. There is Calvary Chapel, the place where the SON shines in phenomenal glory.

At first glance the Chapel's red tile roof, arched portals and early California architecture resemble an affluent real estate office. It seems logical. The Chapel is located in an upper middle-class housing development on the borders of Costa Mesa and Santa Ana. But this is no ordinary church building. It is almost an hour before the seven o'clock service and the parking lot is filling up! Most of the cars seem to be Volkswagens and almost all wear orange, red and green bumper stickers—*Things go better with Jesus, Have a nice forever, Honk if you love Jesus.*

There's a modest sign on a crew-cut lawn. In clear simple lettering it reads, CALVARY CHAPEL, JESUS CHRIST IS LORD, ADORE HIM WITH US. And those who go inside do.

It's still early. The ushers smile, hand out bulletins and point to the few remaining seats. The main one-thousand-capacity sanctuary is almost full and another four to five hundred sit outside on the stone patio on folding chairs.

The din is almost overpowering but it isn't the eruption and disorder of a political rally. It is the sound that comes from good friends together at a large banquet hall; not clamorous or boisterous but good-natured and friendly. The noise isn't bothersome because there is an instant warmth. The warmth you feel when you are touched by someone who loves you very much.

The unique blending of two generations is obvious. Young girls with shiny blond waist-length hair dressed in T-shirts and cut-offs sit beside and share Scripture verses with two white-haired ladies. Two girls walk in. One, with large dangling earrings, is dressed in an ankle-length peasant dress. Her companion wears hot pink shorts with a purple top and an Indian embroidered tote bag. Both sit next to a young man in brown cords and beige colored desert boots. He wears a button down shirt and neatly clipped blond hair. Three young bearded men with hair to their shoulders and bare feet sit quietly and reverently reading their Bibles.

All of a sudden the noise stops like someone flicking a switch. Every eye is focused on the platform. Some hear him before they see him, Chuck Smith, pastor of Calvary Chapel. His voice is clear and concise as he opens in prayer.

"Lord, we're grateful for having this opportunity to gather and share Your Word together . . ." The prayer ends and without prior announcement Chuck begins to sing in a rich, baritone voice.

"I will bless the Lord at all times . . ." The melody is vibrant and the entire congregation stands. Young and old together link arms and gently sway as they sing with him. "His praise shall continually be in my mouth . . ."

The unaccompanied harmony is beautiful, powerful, almost celestial. It's impossible not to adore the Lord because love bounces off the walls.

". . . Oh, magnify the Lord with me, and let us exalt His name together . . ." There is no fanfare, no song leader and no hymnbook. They don't need them. Everyone holds a Bible and they sing the psalms.

"Before we study our chapters in Luke," Chuck says, "there are some great things happening over at Corona del Mar High School with their football team and I've asked Mike to share them with us."

The young man is shy, soft spoken and wears a wine colored Hang Ten T-shirt and wheat colored cords. He begins his story. "A Christian guy on the Corona del Mar team felt burdened to pray for his kinda wild coach named Dave. He really wanted Dave to get born again. Well, one day our paths cross and I find out Dave has become a Christian and is having prayer meetings before every game. Dave's really enjoying this season with the Lord.

"During a game against Newport, Corona got the ball and ran sixty-three yards for a winning touchdown. After the game the guys and girls carried Dave off the field and Dave was smiling and making the One Way sign with his finger. Most of the kids thought he meant his team was number one. So a couple of players yelled, 'Praise the Lord! Jesus saves!' When I saw Dave after the game I said, 'Gee Dave, that was really beautiful, man.' And Dave said, 'Yeah, I know. In the last game I learned I was trying too hard on my own. This game I just asked Jesus to help me call the plays and, man, He really did!' "

"Praise God," said Chuck. "Dave has a beautiful ministry ahead of him. Now let's see what Dr. Luke has to say to us."

Immediately people adjust and shift their positions like children getting ready to hear their favorite story. All open their Bibles and for an instant there is a rustle of onionskin Bible paper. One final survey of the sanctuary and patio reveals every seat is filled with almost no air space between shoulders of those sitting in the richly stained upholstered pews. People without seats have snuggled down comfortably on the green shag aisle rugs. The face of each person, the straights and those representing the youth culture, is eager and attentive.

Chuck's words are clear, full-bodied and nonthreatening. "Your position in heaven will be relative to the faithfulness to whatever God has called you to do now. It's important to understand that we

4

can't do any more than what God has called us to do . . ." Like a trip-hammer Chuck begins in Luke 6 and uncovers truth after truth.

"Put everything you've got into running this race with Jesus. Give it your full effort. Be full on for Jesus in every area of your life. If you have come here tonight and feel handicapped or have blown it, don't worry. Peter blew it. He disappointed God. But he repented, came back to God in faith and God accepted him."

The truths, though centuries old, are fresh and new. Many mark and underline their Bibles with felt pens. Chuck preaches for an hour and goes through five chapters of Luke. But he still has more to say and no one seems tired. At one point Chuck departs from his message and tells the congregation he has some interesting truths about Judas but says they will have to wait until they get into John 12 to find out what it is. Immediately a reverent disappointed "Ah-h-h" sweeps the room. Chuck continues to speak for another thirty-five minutes.

"God never called us to judge or condemn others. Even those who make us unhappy with the way they dress . . . And to those of you who are saved and feel you should sit and wait around until the Lord comes, that's negative. Jesus said, 'Occupy till I come.' God never calls anyone to indolence or laziness. Paul dealt with this problem in Thessalonians. He said, 'Listen, if a man doesn't work, he shouldn't eat.' There is nothing unspiritual about working and providing honestly in the sight of all men. Remember, God has given each of us special talents and He will add more to us if we're faithful

5

The truths, though centuries old, are fresh and new. Many make notes and underline their Bibles as Chuck teaches a personal application of God's Word.

in using them. But if we're lazy and unfaithful even the little talent we have will be taken away."

Chuck is forthright and gives honest instruction to the congregation and then in an instant turns the light of Scripture on himself.

"I used to go to conventions and preaching missions and be part of the syndrome of outdoing my colleagues with long flowery introductions. You know, 'How privileged we are to have so-and-so because he's such a great man, etc.' I say that kind of trip is an abomination. It's exalting the flesh rather than exalting Jesus Christ. Now when I'm called to speak and people ask me for something to use as an introduction I just say, 'Chuck Smith, a servant of Jesus Christ.' That's good enough. That's all I want to be. Hang the eulogy! If anything has been wrought here at Calvary Chapel it's been done and is being done by Jesus Christ and the work of the Holy Spirit. What a privilege to stand here and watch Him work! That's so glorious!"

A wave of fifteen hundred uplifted arms with extended index fingers fills the air—a silent response of gratefulness and praise to God for the freedom they have found to say, "Hang the eulogy. Christ is all we need!"

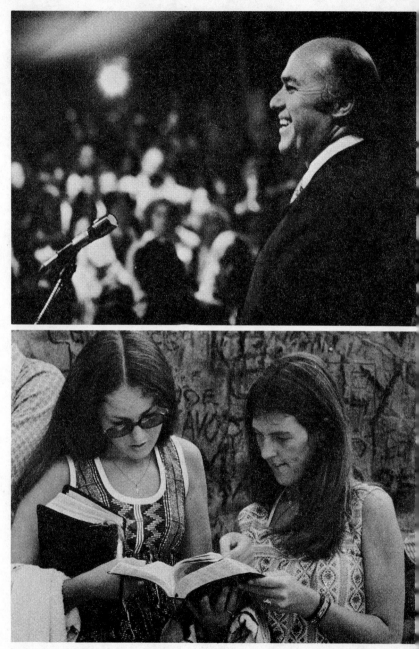

Love and joy, sharing and caring, radiate from the faces of Pastor Smith and those who gather to praise the Lord and study in the Word of God together.

CHAPTER TWO

About-Face

His suits are conservative browns, greens or dark blue with matching ties of subdued flowers and prints. His voice is husky and reassuring. He's bald with a long curly version of a Brother Sebastian fringe. In his mid-forties, the Reverend Charles Smith looks like a successful high school principal, football coach or a favorite uncle.

That success has come to Chuck Smith and Calvary Chapel is obvious. But why and how the success has come are questions being asked by churchmen all over the world. Recently delegates from Switzerland, England and the Philippines came to the little tile-roofed chapel to find the so-called patterns for success.

"Funny thing," says Chuck. "When they ask about this I feel like a bystander. I remind them it's not Chuck Smith at work. It's God through His Holy Spirit turning people on."

Those who come regularly to Calvary Chapel agree with their pastor and give full praise to God. But they also enthusiastically contend there are measurable reasons for Calvary's unique success.

Lee Hayes, an attractive dark-haired widow and mother of two pre-teen girls said, "I visited Calvary and stayed because the main object was getting into the Word."

Then she laughed with the excitement of being able to articulate her feelings. "It's fabulous! People here look at each other through Christ's eyes and are respected and accepted for what they are. It's the most non-judgmental church I've ever been in. And I believe that's the way Christ wants us to live!"

Wilson Stiteler sports a handsome white Vandyke beard, works as a home-assigned executive for Wycliffe Bible Translators and attends Calvary regularly.

"My wife and I go," he said, "because Chuck always gives us practical teaching we can use and think about. There's an unusual air of reverence and expectancy and a feeling that the Lord is really working in our midst.

"During one of our first services at Calvary we were ushered to a seat beside two barefoot youths. Quietly and politely one turned to the other and said, 'Make some room. Here's a brother coming.' We find the kids eager to learn from anyone, young or old, who will share a truth or blessing from the Word."

Susie Hendry is a nineteen-year-old fresh-faced strawberry blond and strong Calvary Chapel devotee. Like many of Calvary's teenagers, Susie comes from a conservative middle-class American family. She lives with her parents in a quiet suburb of Santa Ana, wears ankle length dresses, has a part-time job, teaches Sunday school at Calvary and sings and plays her guitar regularly at the Orange County Jail chapel services. She drives a Volkswagen convertible with a red dash sticker which says, "If you hear a trumpet blast, grab the wheel. The driver of this car is saved."

Susie's reasons for joining Calvary are typical. "I accepted Jesus during my junior year at high school. But when I started telling people about Him, I just didn't feel I had anything to give. I never knew what it was that made me different and most people seemed as happy or happier than I. I started to drift away and I knew inside I wasn't right with God.

"In 1968 at the Billy Graham Crusade, I became a counselor. My mom thought the instruction class would do me good. When I went to the class I just sat back and listened in a halfhearted way. Then one day during the training class I began to think about my life and I said, 'God, I know You're there but for some reason You're not real to me anymore and I don't know why. If You really want to use me, please do something in my heart.' And He did! But when I tried to share Christ with others, most of the kids at my church didn't seem interested. I'd want to read the Bible and sit through Sunday school and learn something. But the kids just wanted to pass notes, giggle, chew gum and talk. I thought, well, wow! If this is church, man, I don't even want it.

11

"Then one night my girl friend and I visited a Christian commune house we'd heard about called The Miracle House. We knocked at the door and a hippie long-haired type answered and invited us in. This was my first experience with this kind of person and I was kind of startled. He started talking about the Lord. He looked like a hippie but he was really right on!

"He told us about Calvary Chapel and invited us to come. We did and I've been going ever since. I found a broad area of personal involvement that I never had before. Calvary Chapel really meets my needs just like it meets the needs of the four to five thousand people who come each Sunday."

A newly converted young man in his early twenties explained what Calvary's ministry was doing in his life. "I left my home in Springfield, Massachusetts, when I was thirteen," he said. "Since then I've been going through trials alone. I never opened or shared my heart with anyone. But now I have Christ and I know there is power in prayer for any trial I face. I also have the brothers and sisters at Calvary. I can grow and pray with them. I remember I used to worry what I was going to do with my life. Now I am happy just to live for the Lord day by day. Man, it's great to know He'll guide me to do what I'm supposed to do.

"It was like that when the Lord brought me to Calvary Chapel. I had heard about it but had forgotten where it was. Then a Christian fellow picked me up when I was hitchhiking one day and brought me to Mansion Messiah, a Christian commune, and then to Calvary Chapel. I'm so blessed to be here!

It's not just the singing and fellowship. It's the way
the Bible is presented. You know we're assigned a
certain part of the Bible to read—like five chapters.
That way the whole church reads it together during
the week. Then on Sunday Pastor Chuck preaches
on it. It's really a fruitful ministry."

Recently this young man went back to Springfield to share his new faith with his non-Christian
parents. "When I got back home," he said, "my
mom just couldn't believe it. She couldn't get over
the change. She knew I had been up on LSD, in
and out of jail and wandering all over the country.
'I don't know what it is,' she said. 'But there's something different about you. There's something in
your eyes that wasn't there before.'"

Chuck, with his attractive wife Kay, and their
four children, Jan, Chuck Jr., Jeff and Cheryl, came
to Calvary Chapel in 1965 as assistant pastor. The
move caused Kay to seriously doubt her husband's
ability to make sound judgment.

"After all," she said, "why would he want to leave
our work in Corona, California. It was a growing
congregation of over one hundred fifty. The people
loved us. We had an important radio ministry and
Chuck left it all to be second man to a dwindling
congregation of twenty-five."

But this was not the first time "Daddy Chuck," as
the youth affectionately call him, left the comfort-
able security of an established work to pioneer a
new or smaller charge. After junior college in Santa
Ana and graduating from Life Bible School in Los
Angeles, Chuck and Kay began their denominational ministry in Prescott and Tucson, Arizona.

They accepted calls to Corona, Huntington Beach, Los Seranos and Costa Mesa in southern California.

It was during his Costa Mesa pastorate that Chuck, after almost seventeen years in the ministry, did an about-face. "I just came to the place," he said, "where I could no longer digest the stifling restrictive role I was required to play. I felt the endless competitive records, program charts for development and membership drives did not really serve to build up believers nor extend Christ's kingdom. There never seemed to be room for the Holy Spirit to work creatively among us."

Chuck and Kay began by opening up their newly purchased home in Newport Beach to small Bible study groups.

"I started these," Chuck said, "because I felt I could accomplish more in one evening of informal relaxed study than I could in three thirty-minute services standing behind a lectern. I found that without the folderol of opening announcements, songs and offering that I could teach for an hour to an hour and a half or even two hours and have the complete attention of my audience. Most of the forty to fifty people who came found that sitting and talking informally was a new and exciting way to get into the Word. And I found it was a most successful way to reach and train people."

And successful it was! Within eighteen months after Chuck began, he not only had his own Newport Beach study group and Costa Mesa pastorate, but had started five more home Bible study groups. His weekly schedule looked like the itinerary of a mad-scramble-first-time tourist to California. Laguna Beach on Monday, Corona on Tuesday, Costa Mesa church prayer meeting Wednesday, Newport on Thursday, San Clemente on Friday and once a month at West Covina.

Many of the people who came to the studies week by week were from established churches but admitted that for years they had only half listened to the litanies or meaningless Latin words or to the battered cliches of an egotistical preacher. Suddenly, all of them found an exhilarating excitement in the pure uncluttered study of God's Word.

One young couple who attended the Newport Beach study said, "We got good preaching in our own church. But that's what it was—preaching! My wife and I were longing to hear someone just expound the Word itself in clear positive terms and Chuck's expositional studies were just that."

Churchgoers of many years discovered the compelling truths of Romans, Hebrews, Revelation and other books. What had for years been unexplored territory now became new, familiar and instructive.

By September of 1964 the home Bible studies became so large and demanding that Chuck resigned his Costa Mesa pastorate to give the home study program his full attention.

"It was a hard step of faith," said Chuck. "But for the first time in many years I no longer felt I was playing at church. I knew God had equipped me naturally to be a teacher. I saw the need and knew in my heart I was doing at that moment what God wanted."

When the Bible study group in Corona knew Chuck had resigned his pastorate in Costa Mesa, they invited him to hold Sunday services in the Corona American Legion Hall. The Corona group grew beyond Chuck's highest expectations. Just a few weeks before the group invited Chuck they said, "We are being so enriched by the Word we feel it's wrong and selfish to keep the good things to ourselves." The group then formed into the Corona Christian Association. Many of the families began to tithe and look for an effective outreach ministry. They began with a daily fifteen-minute Bible study over Corona's local KREL radio station. Within two weeks, the Tuesday night class was crowded out.

"After that," said one member, "it seemed only natural to invite Chuck permanently."

Feeling this was God's timing, Chuck moved his family and base of operations to Corona. He thought about selling the Newport home but decided instead to lease when friends said they would like to buy it after they sold their home. In the meantime, the Smiths bought what Kay described as her perfect dream house. Then to supplement his income Chuck helped a friend in construction build a motel, and later taught school.

Chuck's schedule was now busier than ever. Yet with all the trauma of buying a house, getting settled and conducting Bible studies every night, the Corona Christian Center showed remarkable growth. The once-a-week home Bible study group that started with three couples had, in eighteen months, grown to a strong church of over one hundred fifty. The Center outgrew the American Legion Hall and moved across the street to a large community women's club auditorium.

Perhaps it was their strength and rapid growth that caused Chuck to consider a move back to Newport Beach. "I really can't explain it," said Chuck, "but I began to feel a tug inside back to the beach area. I would drive by our old house which we were still leasing and wish we were back in it even though our house in Corona was much nicer. I still had a home study group in Costa Mesa and they were encouraging me to come back and offered support if we did."

Then one day Chuck met the contractor with whom he had worked and he told Chuck about Calvary Chapel.

"We're having a whole lot of problems," he said. "Our present pastor doesn't seem to be too interested in pastoring the work like he should. We only have about twenty-five on Sunday morning and consider ourselves lucky if six to twelve come out on Sunday night. I know God has blessed you in Corona but I wonder if you would consider moving to a new ministry."

"Yes," said Chuck with a broad smile. "I don't know why but, strange as it may seem, I would be interested. However, I don't know what my wife will say about this!"

A personal relationship with a living Lord becomes real for the many people who seek Christ through Bible study and times of praise, prayer and worship.

CHAPTER THREE

The Doll's House

"Chuck Smith! I'm your wife and if I think you're crazy, so will everyone else. It's utter foolishness to think about moving back to Newport Beach. We've only been here a little over a year and that . . . that Calvary Chapel," sputtered Kay, "is full of all kinds of problems. The kind we don't need! The church here in Corona is going great. We're fitting into the community. For the first time in our life we have a house to be proud of. What more could you want? I just don't think you really appreciate what God has done for you!"

"Look, honey," said Chuck as tenderly as he could. "I know how you feel. But the work here is now strong enough to stand alone. I just can't explain why, but I feel drawn back to the beach areas."

Several weeks and debates later, Kay reluctantly approached her husband one night after his return from a study class. "Honey," she said with a sigh, "I've been praying about things. And the Lord has impressed upon me that my position must be one of submission to you. And although I think you are absolutely crazy, I'll submit!"

"Wow!" beamed Chuck. "That's really great! I'm so thankful and appreciate your position, honey, because the board at Calvary contacted me yesterday!"

"Look," blurted Kay, "don't talk to me about it anymore! I'm not ready to move yet. All I'm ready to do is submit."

When Kay finally understood the terms under which her husband accepted the call, she knew he wasn't rational. "I just can't understand," she would say, "why you would accept the call to be an assistant pastor when you have the complete responsibility in Corona." Chuck would remind his wife again that he felt the Lord leading him and as His servant it was his duty to obey.

Then two small miracles happened that seemed to confirm Chuck's action. The first occurred shortly after the lease on their Newport Beach house expired and the tenants moved out. The friends who originally planned to buy the house when Chuck and Kay moved to Corona called. "We're ready to buy your house," they said. "Ours finally came out of escrow two days ago."

"I'm sorry, old friend," said Chuck good-naturedly, "but we've decided to move back."

"Praise the Lord!" said his friend. "We've been praying for you and Kay to come back. Now I know why our escrow was held up. God was just holding your house for your move back!"

The second miracle occurred on the very first Sunday Chuck came to hold services at Calvary. Because Kay was still reluctant to show their Corona house to prospective buyers, Chuck bought a dime store "For Sale" sign and quietly tacked it on the garage. But Kay saw him and asked what he was doing.

"Oh," said Chuck innocently, "I figured we could put up a sign while we're gone and see what happens."

When they returned that night, the Smiths found a card in the front door. "I am very interested in your house. Please call."

Chuck called and the voice on the other end of the line said, "I'm an American Airlines pilot and I've got a flight out in the morning. But my wife would like to come out tomorrow at noon."

"Fine," said Chuck, "send her out."

The woman and her mother arrived promptly the following noon, took one look through the house, sat down and wrote out a deposit check. "Here," she said. "I want to buy your house."

Chuck began his ministry at Calvary Chapel on a cold bright December morning in 1965. The Chapel, once the handsomest church building in Costa Mesa, was now one of the oldest and looked it. The once sparkling white paint that had shone proudly in the California sun, was now dull, cracked and peeling. When people walked in, the stained pine floors squeaked in agonizing protest.

"It just seemed that no one cared about the little church," said Chuck. "There were cobwebs in the corners, a nursery window off to one side with dirty drapes and an open baptistry with a not-too-professional mural painted on the inside. The woodwork that came up to the wide window casings was heavy and dull."

But in spite of the gloomy setting Chuck was enthusiastically optimistic. And after the first morning service and special luncheon, so was the small band of believers.

Marlene and Glenn Jackson remember Chuck's remarks with delight. "He told us," said Marlene, "that before next Sunday he wanted all of us to read the first ten chapters of Genesis because he was going to give an expository message from these chapters. And in the evening would review and analyze the same ten chapters. He said that as long as he was our pastor this would be the format of his Sunday services.

"I thought this was new and different," said Marlene, "and I was inwardly glad for the opportunity to study the Scriptures in depth. I had gone to church all my life and felt the Bible was in many ways a closed book. For the first time in my Christian life I began to apply the Word and make Christianity work in every area of my life."

That first afternoon Chuck and most of the Calvary membership met in a nearby restaurant for lunch. In words that were never threatening or coercive, Chuck shared his Bible study outline, his plan to remodel the sanctuary, especially the platform, and something of his own philosophy.

"I believe," he said, "that man has only one problem. His relationship to God. If man is fully committed to seeking God's kingdom and His righteous-

A shared love of Jesus brings together the youth culture and the establishment. Group singing, study and fellowship help build strong foundations for new life.

ness first, then problems, frustrations, the strivings for recognition, popularity, you-name-it, will disappear.

"I look at man as having a vertical and horizontal axis to his life. The vertical represents man's living relationship to God through personal faith in Jesus Christ. The horizontal represents man's interpersonal relationships. If our vertical axis is straight our horizontal axis will also be straight and in balance. But if the vertical relationship is off balance, so will be the horizontal, and our day to day life becomes a purposeless drag or frantic round of activity. I discovered a right vertical relationship produces unbelievable strength and grace to cope with all the stress factors of life.

"The home Bible study programs showed me," continued Chuck, "that Christians, some of whom have known the Lord for many years and believe the Bible, have never really read it through or taken its instruction seriously. I find when these people begin consistently to read and study the Word a new excitement comes into their lives and things happen they never dreamed possible. This is the reason why I began in Genesis this morning. If we cover ten chapters each Sunday and fifteen chapters when we come to the Psalms we can go through the whole Bible in two years.

"Now, regarding the sanctuary. Most of us would not live in quarters as dismal as our little church. I believe if we remodel the platform, put in paneling, indirect lighting and carpet the squeaking floors we'll see some startling changes."

A week later the changes began. True to form

Chuck began a local Monday night home Bible study in Revelation. On the heels of this came a Wednesday night study in the Epistle of First John in Huntington Beach and Romans was studied on Thursday night at the church. From previous experience Chuck knew that many non-Christians found church a bore, uncomfortable, or totally irrelevant to their everyday needs. Chuck also knew that studying the Scriptures in an easy informal atmosphere of a home would interest people and open up the neighborhood in a positive manner.

Six months after that first luncheon get-together, Calvary Chapel doubled its membership and painted and remodeled the entire church. What had once been a ramshackle building that people hurried past, was now a beautiful attractive chapel. "It looked," said one person, "like a little doll's house."

In the next six months Calvary's membership doubled again. In eighteen months the little chapel that began with twenty-five people was completely crowded out with 120 to 150 regular attenders. And by the end of 1967 Chuck and the Calvary board began thinking about property to build a larger church facility.

"It was a predictable repeat of what happened in Corona," said Chuck. "People came to the home Bible studies, got turned on and came to church for further instruction and fellowship."

A survey of the people who swelled Calvary's ranks that first year showed an interesting statistic. About half were unchurched. The other half were churchgoers but confided they lacked the spiritual dynamic for effective Christian growth. They were

well-thought-of-citizens from a strong, well mani-
cured middle and upper middle-class white Anglo-
Saxon community—a president of a large real estate
developing company, an oral surgeon, teachers,
business executives, top sales personnel, artists. And
there was John Nicholson, a thin-faced young man
with bright blue eyes, horn-rimmed glasses and
neatly clipped long blond hair. Normally John
would have caused more than a passing interest
among the people at Calvary by just being Jan's
boyfriend. But John was more than just a young
man the pastor's daughter brought home from college. He was for many, including Chuck, their first
close contact with the youth drug and hippie culture. John had lived and gone through the confusion
and horror of Haight-Ashbury; but found the
Lord through the witness of people from the San
Francisco commune, House of Acts.

"I wish you would bring a real hippie home
sometime," said Chuck one day to John. "I am interested in their whole philosophy. I want very
deeply to understand their life style and what they
are trying to say."

In a few months John would bring in a strange
mixture of new people to be fed the incredible
Bread of Life. But for now, God, through Chuck's
ministry, was still building the strong foundations
that would support this great responsibility.

During this season of rapid growth, the previous
pastor, who had been retained as minister of visita-
tion, resigned. The board realistically faced the
problem of a larger sanctuary and made several
building proposals.

26

The property selected was two thirds of an acre on Bay Street behind a Ford agency in Costa Mesa. There wasn't room for parking but a happy arrangement was worked out to use the agency's parking lot on Sundays.

Everything was set. The Costa Mesa City Planning Department reviewed the architectural blueprints and was well pleased as were most of Calvary's members. Those who opposed the move were out-voted and it was decided to sell. The doll house chapel sold for cash three days after it was advertised.

To give themselves time to build a new facility the board put the chapel into a six-month escrow. Fewer negotiations had worked smoother or easier. But for the minority and some on the planning committee it all seemed too easy. "And besides," they told Chuck one day, "the Bay Street property does not fit the description of the prophecy."

"Prophecy?" questioned Chuck. "What prophecy?"

"Before you accepted the call to Calvary," they said, "we were planning to close the doors of Calvary Chapel and call it quits. But one of our church members said we shouldn't do this. The Lord told him you would accept the call to be our pastor. He said when you came you would not be satisfied with the church building and would want to remodel, especially the platform. You do remember how unhappy you were with the platform when you first came."

"Yes," answered Chuck, "I do. And what you have told me is all very interesting. But there is always a human element and prophecy is to be judged."

"That may be true," said the committee. "But we know the first part came true."

"First part?" said Chuck.

"Yes," they said, "there is more. This man also said Calvary Chapel would move to a new location overlooking the bay. And that the Chapel would one day be known nationwide."

"Did any of you notice," said Chuck, "that the new church property is on Bay Street?"

"No," said the committee, "that's not what the prophecy said. It was to be on a bluff overlooking the bay."

Chuck rubbed his thick hand over his bald head and smiled. "Totally impractical," he said.

In Chuck's mind this was indeed a totally impractical suggestion. In the first place he never in all his ministry aspired for personal fame. Repeatedly he stressed the concept of pastor and layman being equal. "We are colaborers together," he would say. "God calling me as a pastor doesn't make my calling greater or more important than God calling you to be a businessman, teacher or laborer. We all share equally in our ministries as members of the body of Christ. In addition all of us will give an account, not to man but to God, on how well we dispatch our responsibilities."

When Chuck said these things, his friends and members of the congregation knew he had never tried to put himself above other people. Rather than preach messages, harangue or pontificate, Chuck shared truths and promises choosing to be the same person in the pulpit as he was at the dinner table.

Chuck knew the prophecy was impractical when the city planning commission in a later meeting decided against the Bay Street property because of the inadequate parking. They felt if the agency ever sold to a new owner they could rescind the parking privilege. Now unable to find a suitable substitute the board faced the additional problem of the six-month escrow running out.

But before it did, a woman in the city planning department told Chuck of a Lutheran church which planned to vacate their premises. "The state bought the property for a new freeway site," she said. "If you see the right people you might be able to move in when they move out or even share their premises at a different hour. I've heard it will be several years before the freeway will actually be built. I know you'll love the church. It's right on Tustin Avenue and Cliff Drive in Newport Beach. The view is really great. It's right on the bluff overlooking the bay."

Beautiful faces reflect the peace, love and joy of people who have found freedom in the Christian life and who are growing according to God's plan.

CHAPTER FOUR

Striving Is Not Where It's At

"When I first saw Chuck I couldn't believe it. He was sitting on a folding chair on the platform talking to the people. Just explaining or translating the Scriptures into everyday Christian principles. My wife, Bev, and I sat there like thirsty children. Our spirits and our very flesh absorbing the fresh workable truths, like water pouring into dry sand. The following Sunday we found ourselves wanting to go back. Really wanting to go back!"

What Dempster and Bev Evans experienced during their first Sunday morning at Calvary was the end of what they termed a "squirrel cage environment." Dempster, a highly talented freelance graphic artist, and his wife are, by their own admission, a little avant-garde. Their early Christian life in North Hollywood was normal, almost staunch, with few ups and downs. As they grew older they began to experience a hunger for relevancy in their Christian and church life. "We would attend church and afterward have the temptation to become critical," said Dempster. "Mostly because we kept doing the same thing over and over. Three hymns, choir number, announcements, message. Like a squirrel running around and around in a cage.

"Our inter-church activity was a traditional striving and concern for membership and Sunday school contests. But the striving was not so that we could reach out and touch people where they were hurting or to meet non-Christians as real people. Our striving was to get people in through the church doors and I began to understand that striving is not where it's at! Things I wanted to see happen in the church were not coming about naturally. I discovered when people are truly excited about their Lord and fellowship, the church becomes a rallying point instead of a come-sit-listen society. Then the striving for numbers, money and recognition falls away because people are moving close to the Word of God and the promise, 'If I be lifted up I will draw all men unto me.' And that is where it is at!"

The Evans moved from North Hollywood in early 1968 to Orange County. With the change of geography they decided not to make a firm church commitment until they discovered what people in the area were saying, doing and thinking.

Several months after their arrival Bev was invited to a bridal shower and ran into a former school chum who asked her if she had ever heard of Calvary Chapel. Bev said no but was interested since they were looking for a new church home.

"It's really great," said her friend. "Right now we are holding services in a rented Lutheran church in Newport Beach. We meet in the afternoon after their morning service. It's fantasttic the way the church is growing. We even have a few hippie types who come!"

"I don't know if I would like that," said Bev with a light laugh.

"Oh," said her friend, "we just have two or three and they are very kind and lovely people."

"But what kind of program do you have," asked Bev, "to generate such enthusiasm and interest?"

"That's the neat thing," said her friend. "We really don't have a program. We have some great singing but it's the Bible studies that pull it all together. It's kind of hard to explain. But when you and Dempster come to hear Chuck Smith teach, you'll know what I mean!"

Attending Calvary became a totally new and exciting experience for the Evans. For years Sunday morning had been a scramble—hurry up out of the bathroom, let's get going, we're late for church experience. The afternoon service at Calvary was great. They knew when Calvary moved from the Lutheran church to a new facility they would go back to the traditional morning hour. But for now they enjoyed a leisurely Sunday morning where they could have brunch, read the Word together and go off to church relaxed, prepared in mind, body and soul.

When Chuck and the people at Calvary moved to the Lutheran church in March of 1968 they accepted it as a temporary provision of the Lord. But then some began to talk of using the facility for a longer period of time, as much as five or six years. At first it was inconvenient for some to meet in the afternoon but the Lutherans were happy to have the Calvary folk use the building and for a while it looked like this facility was the Lord's choice for Calvary Chapel.

Then in April Chuck received a letter from the Santa Ana school district. "Dear Reverend Smith," it read. "This is to advise you that the old Greenville School on the corner of Greenville and Sunflower in Santa Ana is being declared surplus property and will be open for bid." The letter then gave the date and terms under which bids would be handled.

Chuck laughed and shook his head. Months before when they were looking for property Chuck had driven past the old school and noticed it wasn't being used. The main building was in early California architecutre and Chuck thought it could easily be converted to a church or Sunday school. When he asked the school board if the property was for sale they said no, but didn't quite know what they were going to do with it. "If you ever declare it surplus property," said Chuck, "let me know." And in April they did.

At the end of the Calvary board meeting later that month, Chuck casually suggested there was one small item of business they should probably consider. "I forgot all about the Greenville School property," he said, "but if you're interested it might be a good investment. Property in this area sells for $60,000 an acre. The school board is opening the bid at $53,000 for an acre and six tenths. And it has a building!"

"We have $38,000 in the bank," said one of the board members, "why don't we submit a minimum bid and see what happens."

Chuck and the board were so convinced they would not get the Greenville property that on the day it was offered for open bid, they didn't attend. The following morning Chuck received a call from the secretary of the school board. "Well," he said, "it looks like you folks purchased the Greenville School last night. Would you please come over and make the necessary escrow arrangements."

Hardly believing the secretary's words, Chuck laid the receiver back into its cradle. "Oh, Lord," he thought, "I guess You really do want us to move out there. I wonder what You have in mind for us."

At a hastily called membership meeting it was decided to proceed immediately with plans to build. There was a moment of hesitancy, however, when the Calvary board discovered the savings and loan company would lend the remaining $15,000 at 10 percent plus ten points.

In casual conversation with his Jewish boss, the owner of a large southern California business, a member of Calvary's board mentioned the high interest rates.

"That's outrageously high interest to charge a church," responded the owner. "I'll be happy to loan you the $15,000 interest free."

Most of the people were happy with the new property. Some who lived in Newport were a little disappointed because it meant a longer drive.

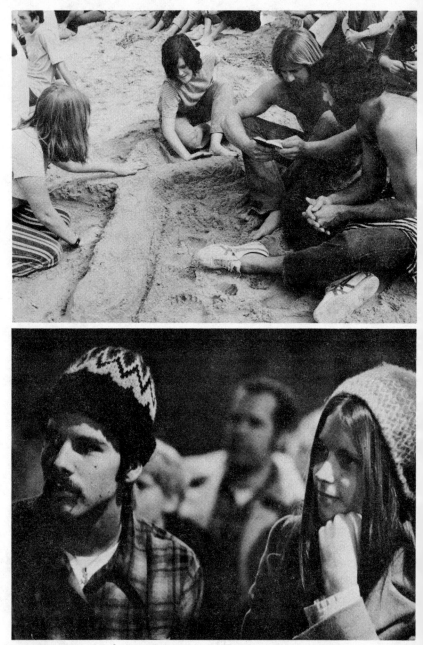

Spirit-led witnessing and Christlike love brought a new ministry to the little suburban church with hippies, drug addicts and other lost and lonely youth.

Chuck and Kay lived only six blocks from the Lutheran church but Chuck concluded that as a servant of Christ it was his duty to obey and follow the leading of his Master.

"In strife, opposites combine to produce a motion called harmony," so wrote Greek philosopher Heraclitus. But the combination of opposites that occurred during Calvary's months at the Lutheran church and the following years came not from strife but from love. It was love that prompted John Nicholson to spend his free time on the beach witnessing. And it was not uncommon for him to lead two or three young drug users to the Lord in an afternoon. "I was talking to five kids who were stoned on acid," he said to Chuck one day, "and the Spirit used me to speak to them and all were converted."

It was the same love and desire to witness that prompted John to pick up a hitchhiking hippie one night and begin sharing his testimony with him.

The hitchhiker let John speak for a few minutes then reached into his pocket and pulled out a Bible. "Far out, man," he said. "I'm a Christian too. I was just hitchhiking so I could witness to anyone who would pick me up."

"Hey," said John, "that's great. Say, I wonder if you would like to meet some friends of mine. They've been wanting to meet a hippie for a long time. Man, when they see you with your beard and long hair and find out you're a Christian carrying a Bible, it'll blow their minds! By the way, my name's John. What's yours?"

"Lonnie," he said. "Lonnie Frisbee."

John and Lonnie knocked on the Smith's door later that evening. What the Smiths saw and felt almost did blow their minds! Not because they couldn't equate Christians with beards and long hair. But because they saw in this almost frail young man an unusual character and capacity to love. "This might be the very person to help us begin reaching the great numbers of hippies who are migrating to the beach areas," mused Chuck.

As the evening progressed Chuck shared his dream with Lonnie and John. "If you could help John and a few of us share Christ with the hippies on the beach," said Chuck, "I believe they would respond. You speak their language and you know better than any of us how, what and why they think and feel the way they do. Furthermore you could stay with us for a couple of weeks and help me understand what makes them tick."

"I like the idea," said Lonnie, "but I am married and live in San Francisco."

"No problem," said Chuck. "Bring your wife. She can stay too."

In a couple of weeks Lonnie and his wife, Connie, returned and moved in with the Smiths. Several days later two other hippies that Lonnie led to the Lord moved in, and in the true spirit of having all things in common, began to share and help themselves to each others belongings. Connie frequently popped into Jan's closet and borrowed clothes just as if they were her own. But no one in the Smith family resented this. "We were fascinated with their genuine openness and reality," said Kay. "There was so much natural beauty and love bubbling forth we couldn't resist them." And before Lonnie and Connie returned to San Francisco neither could the people at Calvary.

At Chuck's invitation Lonnie told the Calvary congregation one Sunday how he began using drugs in high school. He so zealously believed this was the answer to life's problems he turned on his brothers and most of his friends to drugs. He told of being part of a TV dance show and of winning an art scholarship to study in San Francisco. "But all this really didn't satisfy me," he said. "I studied eastern philosophy and religion. I went through Haight-Ashbury when it was supposed to be where it was at. And then one day some brothers from the House of Acts commune told me where it was really at. And I accepted Jesus Christ. And man, it's true. Jesus is where it's at!"

Lonnie then told how responsible he felt toward those he had influenced into drugs. "I guess I was just like Paul the apostle before he was converted," he said. "I had used all my energy for evil. Now I wanted everyone to meet Jesus Christ and know that He is the only way. And one of the places I started was out in Tahquitz Canyon near Palm Springs. That's where I met Connie. But I'll let her tell you about it."

From a distance she spoke and looked like a young woman who should have been announcing the church's young married couples' next social. Connie brushed her long light brown hair out of her eyes and began to speak. There was warmth in her bright penetrating blue eyes and only occasionally did they betray the hurt of her past. "If you've heard one hippie story you've heard them all," said Connie with a smile, "but Chuck thinks you would be interested in how I found the Lord.

"Tahquitz Canyon up near Palm Springs is beautiful. Lots of trees, waterfalls, rocks—a great place to go on a nature trip. And a great place, or so I thought, to get high on drugs. The canyon is always full of kids who are stoned, having free sex or kids like me who have run away from home. I really didn't have a home from which to run. Mine was all broken up before I left and I had to fight off my mom's boyfriends. The day Lonnie found me I was stoned on acid, lying out on a rock, nude. Just lying there beside a big pool of water. I had known Lonnie from before when he used to come up to the canyon but didn't recognize him at first. All I remember was this guy walking up to me and reading out of the Bible. As he read his voice sort of faded out and God began to speak. 'This is your opportunity now to accept Jesus Christ.' I don't know why but I started to cry. I guess I realized that drugs were a bummer and there was no place else to turn. Through my tears I said I wanted to accept Christ. And I did! Lonnie then asked me if I wanted to be baptized. I said yes. Then just as I was, Lonnie baptized me in the pool. As soon as I was baptized I felt an immediate need to be clothed and I put on a dress. Later as I began to read the Scriptures I came across the story of the demoniac of Gadara and I knew the answer for my action.

"I not only found Christ that day," continued Connie. "I found my husband. Lonnie and I were married several months later."

When Connie finished speaking the church was unusually silent. Few people wanted to speak. What could they say to two young people who had opened their eyes to a world they previously ignored yet existed on their doorstep. They now understood why their pastor was concerned with the growing youth culture problem.

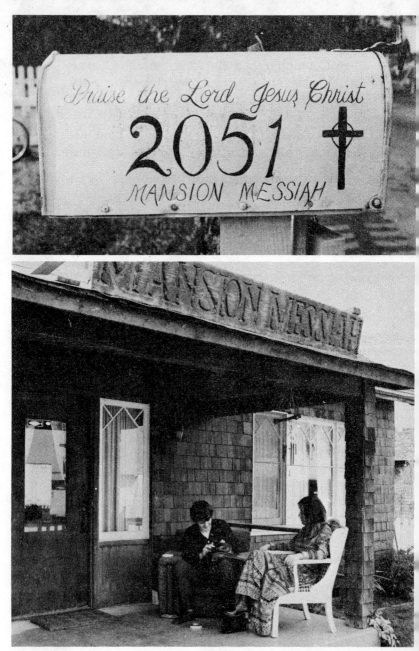

"Praise the Lord" and "Thank You, Jesus" are frequent refrains in the commune houses where new Christians experience the daily excitement of life with Jesus.

CHAPTER FIVE

House of Miracles

"Five hundred dollars isn't much," said a woman to Chuck one day, "but it might be enough to start a program to help young people on drugs."

"Thank you," said Chuck. "But why are you doing this?"

"I have two sons who are drug users," said the woman sadly. "I don't seem to be able to help them. But maybe this little gift will provide the means to help some other mother's son."

Chuck's firsthand knowledge of the drug culture centered on John Nicholson, John and Jackie Higgins, a young Catholic couple who found the Lord at Calvary, and Lonnie and Connie who had returned to San Francisco. Chuck knew the Frisbees had been influenced and helped by the House of Acts commune in San Francisco and thought a similar project in Costa Mesa would be a good beginning.

43

"You are the only person I know with the experience," Chuck said to Lonnie on the long distance phone to San Francisco. "I feel a great urgency to begin a commune house here. We already have money in hand and have rented a two-bedroom house in Costa Mesa. We're calling it the House of Miracles. John Higgins has consented to be the elder and is out every day witnessing on the beach. I wonder if you and Connie would consider praying about coming to join our ministry at Calvary."

By the end of the first week after Lonnie and Connie joined the Calvary staff, twenty-one young men accepted Christ and moved into the House of Miracles.

Lonnie and John spent each day on the beach engaging people in conversation, winning them to the Lord and bringing them to the house. After the evening meal, John and some of the new converts conducted prayer meetings, Bible studies and sharing times. By the end of the second week, almost fifty young people crowded into the house.

They slept wall to wall in the living room, kitchen, bathroom and hallway. Chuck and men from Calvary hastily built bunks in the garage. And after these were filled, kids rolled up in their bedrolls and slept outside in the backyard.

John Higgins quickly rethought the purpose of the commune and said to himself, "If the purpose is to help new Christians get on their feet, then we're doing them a disservice by allowing them to lie around inactive."

Exercising his right of eldership, John called an emergency meeting one night. "All right," he said,

Commune members share Bible study, housekeeping chores, meals, job-hunting problems and the growth of each individual in the promised new life with Christ.

"because you guys have been sitting around we don't have room for any more new converts. Furthermore, you guys have been Christians for two whole weeks. It's time for you to get out and evangelize."

The following morning three young men took John at his word and headed out to Tahquitz Canyon, the same place where Lonnie found Connie. Two of the young men, Jim Golden and Jim Manning, were intimately familiar with the area and knew that because of the large amount of kids who went there to turn on to drugs, they would find a ready mission field.

As they came into the canyon, they walked up to a young girl sitting on a rock and sat down beside her. They introduced themselves and found out her name was Cherise. The fellows noticed she had a Bible, a book on religion and her oats, sometimes known as birdseed which is a mixture of sunflower seeds, raw oats and raisins.

When they began to tell her about Christ, Cherise exclaimed, "Wow! This really blows my mind! I came out here two weeks ago to find God. I finished my book on religion but it didn't turn me on. So I picked up the Bible a little while ago and I prayed, 'Oh God, if You're for real and if this book is Yours, send someone along to tell me about it.' And what happens? You guys come walking along!"

"Wow!" said the fellows excitedly. "You're going to have to come with us because it's really happening down in Costa Mesa. There's a house down there and it's really beautiful. They're all Christians and turned on to Jesus."

With that the young evangelists led Cherise to the Lord and out of the canyon. Since there was no room for her at the House of Miracles, they brought her to the Smith's home. Chuck and Kay rejoiced with Cherise's decision to follow the Lord and asked Neil and Diane Fox, members of Calvary, if they would take her in. For the next three days Cherise spent her days helping in the House of Miracles with the cooking and general housework, then returned to the Fox home in the evening. On the third day Chuck discovered that Cherise was a runaway from Riverside, contacted her mother and sent her home.

The following Saturday Cherise returned to the Smith home with five of her friends. "These kids are druggers," she said. "I used to turn on with them. They're so lost and need help. I brought them down here to get saved."

Carefully Chuck, Lonnie, John and a few others explained the way of salvation and all five girls accepted Christ. The following Saturday Cherise returned like a twentieth century Philip. With her were the five young people from the week before plus seventeen others! "These kids are really messed up," she said. "They're on to drugs and need to find Jesus, too." And all seventeen did!

Chuck, Kay and the others from the House of Miracles and Calvary were completely overwhelmed with Cherise's missionary zeal. But when she returned a third week, Chuck and the others found their joy so overpowering it almost hurt. Her entourage was thirty-five strong!

"You can't believe the drug scene out in Riverside," said Cherise. "We need another Miracle House out there badly."

"The only way I know of getting this," said Chuck, "is to pray and tell God our needs." Then in the simplest of ceremonies, these young, baby Christians, some only three to four days old in the Lord, joined hands and prayed for another House of Miracles.

Later the next week, a woman who worked in the trust department of a Riverside bank happened to tell a judge friend of hers about the Costa Mesa commune. She said she didn't really understand what it was all about but whatever it was it had changed her own problematic son overnight from drugs to Jesus Christ. "In fact," said the mother, "he really isn't the same boy. He reads the Bible every day and wishes they had a commune in Riverside."

"Well," said the judge, "I have an old battered motel that could serve as a commune. It doesn't have electricity but it does have gas and water. If the kids want it they can move in rent free."

Immediately, Jim Manning, nineteen, and Jim Golden, seventeen, now five weeks old in the Lord, were sent to be the elders in the second House of Miracles. Within days the sad, old motel was alive with young inhabitants. Parents of young people who had been helped in the commune ministry became cooperative and helpful. Some donated paint and helped clean and paint the motel. Others noticed the lack of electricity and donated Coleman lanterns. And during all this, the two Jims, Cherise, and others held regular Bible studies and daily witnessiing sessions in Van Buren Park a block away.

Van Buren Park was known to the local police department as the heaviest drug area in Riverside. On any morning they could fill a good sized carton with empty glue tubes whose eight-, nine- and ten-year-old users had thrown away. In addition to the glue tubes, there were discarded amphetamine boxes and evidences of marijuana and acid that were being used by their older companions. It was the young people from this inferno that the Miracle House workers wanted to reach.

The format was simplicity itself. After group and individual prayer and Bible study in the motel, the young people went out to the park in twos and threes. Often they sat and waited until young people came along and engaged them in conversation. Others conducted Bible studies under a tree. Those being witnessed to felt a strong sense of identification. Some conservative observers wondered at the youths' candor but had little to say when at the end of the second week after the house was opened, sixty-five young people were baptized in the motel's old fishpond. The person being baptized sat calmly on the low, red-tile pool edge with his back to the water. Jim then leaned the candidate over backwards into the shallow pool.

For these sixty-five young people who found Christ and entered into the symbolism of His death, burial and resurrection, the fishpond baptistry had more meaning than the most impressive church baptistry!

From the beginning the Riverside commune experienced unusual growth and success. Starting with the two Jims and a handful of new believers, the house quickly grew to fifty, then to seventy and by the end of the summer over five hundred young people had come to meet and personally follow the Lord. The witnessing came from new believers only weeks old and in some cases, just days old in the Lord. But the message was always clear and full of meaning.

"Drugs are a bummer, man," they would say. "They're not where it's at. You know when you come down from that high on acid you can have a real bum experience and all you're doing is destroying yourself. But if you want you can have a high with Jesus Christ that will never quit. It's never a bummer with Christ. Just open your heart and ask Jesus Christ to come in and when you do you'll feel His presence. And, man, that's where it's at. It is just beautiful."

The commune houses in Costa Mesa, Riverside, Huntington Beach and the more than one hundred others that have sprung up from Oregon to Georgia exist to provide a place for the newborn hippie Christian to live, have fellowship and be nurtured in the Lord. It is also a place where each one is encouraged to have a disciplined ministry.

The elders take care of the daily spiritual needs by giving ninety minute or longer in-depth Bible studies. Others engage in full-time street evangelism and witnessing. Some become deacons and wait on tables. Other young people make arrangements with local markets to pick up partially spoiled fruits and vegetables and donated meat. The girls cut out bad spots, trim and prepare the enormous quantities of food.

Each house becomes totally self-supporting with a reenactment of Acts 2:44. Some young people who have cars sign them over to the house. Others work outside at regular jobs and consign their paychecks to the house.

Any young person, as long as he is not destructive, is always welcome to have a meal and stay overnight. Those who want to really search the Scriptures or have an immediate housing need are allowed to spend two weeks at the house without an assigned responsibility. Those who want to commit themselves to the "body" and engage in the commune's ministry can stay as long as they want.

Shortly after the Riverside house opened, two incidents occurred that gave unusual strength to the young people's beginning faith. The first occurred on a very hot morning after the girls discovered their daily supply of milk was sour.

"Since we don't have electricity," said the girls, "we need a frige that runs on gas or something."

"If God provided the house," said Jim and some of the others, "then He can provide a refrigerator." Immediately they joined hands and prayed that God would.

But they never finished because they were interrupted by loud repeated horn honking. Outside the young people saw a truck in the driveway with a happy driver leaning out the window.

"Hey," he said, "I was just driving by and noticed you have six or seven old refrigerators out back. I wonder if you'd trade one for a used commercial gas frige that I have in the truck. I'd be happy to hook it up for you if you could use it."

The second incident occurred one afternoon when a gang of black-jacketed motorcyclists roared into the driveway and began annoying the girls. Sometimes shoulder-length hair gives a false illusion of age. Not with Jim Golden. In spite of his slender six foot frame, he sometimes had a hard time convincing people he was seventeen. But never for a moment did Jim consider his age or physical frailty. In a firm, steady voice with a no-nonsense glint in his eyes, Jim approached the gang leader.

"I'm sorry," said Jim, "but this is a Christian commune house. All of us here love Jesus Christ and believe we must respect and honor girls. You're not acting in a way that would please Jesus. Therefore I must ask you to leave. Before you go though, I want to tell you that God loves you and Jesus died for your sins."

As Jim fearlessly began quoting Scriptures, the gang leader, with a strange nonplused look on his face, slowly backed away toward his bike.

"Don't you know," continued Jim, "that you can have a good life if you turn it over to Jesus? 'God so loved the world that He gave His only begotten Son that whosoever believeth in Him should not perish but have everlasting life'" (John 3:16 KJV).

Jim, smiling now, began to quote other Scripture, but never finished. At this point the gang leader hopped on his bike, whistled for his gang, pumped the starter frantically and roared out of the driveway.

Jim and the others smiled and praised the Lord for His protection. But when the same gang roared in the following afternoon, Jim wondered what was going to happen.

"We've had a meeting," said the gang leader, "and we've decided that we dig you guys. We don't understand you, but we dig you. Our gang voted to be your protectors. There's a lot of mean guys and gangs out here in Riverside and you guys need protection. Don't you know it's dangerous to be out here like you are?"

"Hey," said Jim kindly, "we really appreciate that. But you see, Jesus Christ is our protector. And if we really needed help you guys might not be around. But Jesus Christ is always here. So if you don't mind, we'll just go on and let Jesus be our protector. But you guys are welcome to come and eat or share a Bible study anytime. You are always welcome."

In the days immediately following this incident, the leader of the gang and some of his companions returned and found the Lord. When he did, his response was typical of dozens before him. "Wow! This is great! I wonder if we could invite some guys from Fontana. They're a pretty mean bunch but they need to get in on knowing Jesus."

And the Riverside house praised God for the way He was adding daily such as should be saved. Because not only did the Riverside gang believe but some of the Fontana gang as well. And the Lord further blessed by opening up a small five-acre ranch in Fontana with a nice home and large living room to begin yet another commune.

"Long hair, short hair, some coats and ties," they all come to worship and learn in the new sanctuary where solid Bible teaching results in many changed lives

CHAPTER SIX

No Bare Feet Allowed

When they came in ones or twos, or fives and sixes, they were acceptable. The long hair, tinkling brass bells, faded jeans and bare feet were all a novelty. Besides, who could resist the Frisbees, John and Jackie Higgins, and John Nicholson. Their love was real and as contagious as a child's giggle. And they were becoming as much a part of Calvary as Chuck himself.

It was just that some of the members of Calvary were concerned with the balance of influence between the long hairs and their own children. The regular members at Calvary were sincerely thankful to God for the success the communes were having. But when the young people came to church in larger numbers and sat on the floor during services, there were obvious tensions.

One observer remembers the first few Sundays as

"kind of unnerving." At first they hardly knew what was happening. All they saw was a line of long-skirted girls and bearded fellows in jeans and sandals march in and flop down on the floor in front of the platform.

Some members thought their children would become imitators and let their hair grow long or want to come to church unshaven or in sloppy clothes. Glenn Jackson, a tall, handsome ex-marine sergeant, had difficulty at first meeting the hippies because he didn't understand their world.

"To be honest," he said, "I think most of the people at Calvary didn't accept the way they looked and dressed. But later we just looked right past this because we saw their real characters and felt so much love from them.

"My attitude also changed when I began to remember my own high school days. There was really no comparison. I wasn't half as interested in the things of the Lord as those young people.

"In fact," continued Glenn, "I owe a great deal to the so-called hippie movement at Calvary. It was through the study of I John and other love Scriptures Chuck guided us through that I learned that true love is in deed and truth more than just a word.

"After accepting Christ I picked up church jargon and for years sat like a stone while I was being preached at. It wasn't until my wife and I started to attend Calvary that we became aware of what our daily walk with Jesus was supposed to be. The Lord, through Calvary, has helped us grow and become aware of our bigotry and narrowness.

"I especially remember one evening when the Lord gave me a good polishing. I overheard Lonnie Frisbee introduce two young girls to Kay Smith. 'Isn't it neat,' he said excitedly. 'I picked these girls up when they were hitchhiking and brought them to church. Both girls accepted the Lord this morning!'

"When I saw and heard Lonnie's enthusiasm, love and concern for these girls, I felt about an inch high because I had noticed the girls during the morning service and condemned them in my mind for coming in cut-off jeans and sloppy T-shirts.

"It was things like this that began to shake us up. And as we got further into the Word we saw what the Bible has to say about everyday life. We learned how God was more concerned with what people thought inside than He was with what they wore outside."

There were many like Glenn and his wife at Calvary. Honest people releasing themselves to the guidance of God's Holy Spirit and finding renewed excitement in following Christ. But others found their legalistic backgrounds stiff and unbending and asked Chuck to speak out against the extreme dress and especially the habit the young people had of sitting around on the lawn after church reading their Bibles and smoking.

Chuck responded kindly and with understanding to the older people by saying, "I don't want it ever said that we preach an easy kind of Christian experience at Calvary. But I also don't want to make the same mistake the Holiness church made thirty years ago. Without knowing it they drove out and lost a whole generation of young people with a negative no movie, no dance, no smoke gospel. Let us at Calvary not be guilty of this same mistake. Instead let us trust God and emphasize the work of the Holy Spirit within individual lives. It's exciting and much more real and natural to allow the Spirit to dictate change. Let us never be guilty of forcing our western Christian subculture of clean shaven, short hair or dress on anyone. We want change to come from inside out."

There were also those who criticized Chuck for not speaking out more forcibly against the use of drugs. "We simply declare," answered Chuck, "that drugs, striving to become a millionaire or making sports your whole life is not where it's at. Because the end of all these goals is emptiness and disappointment."

With Chuck's wise counsel, tensions relaxed and the regular members began to see with greater objectivity that the young people were deeply attentive and eager to learn.

"Many of our people were willing to accept the youth culture," said Chuck, "but were confused about their apparent lack of interest in regular employment." But when the youths began to work together with the straights on the Greenville church property, opinions changed.

At first the Calvary membership was disappointed when the building they planned to use for a Sunday school was condemned. But they believed all things work together for good, accepted the fact, and used the materials to build the Chapel.

When they began building the Chapel, the older

men were astounded at the eager willingness with which the young people worked. They were fascinated to see fellows and girls with blistered hands working together all day long, singing choruses, scrubbing and cleaning tile from the old school building. With the long hours of extra work came a greater bond of love and understanding between the generations.

More than one person driving by almost ran off the road in mesmerized disbelief as they watched conventionally attired men working side by side with bearded youths sporting headbands and embroidered shirts.

But even with all this, the battle for acceptance and understanding was still not over. Like the children of Israel who quickly forgot God's blessing after their deliverance, the folks at Calvary forgot their priorities.

"This is a very good shag," said the man who installed the carpeting after Calvary was built, "and the worst thing in the world for it is bare feet. There are oils in the feet which mingle with dirt and make cleaning impossible."

One woman expressed the sentiment of many at Calvary when she spoke up and said, "It was all right for young people to come into the Lutheran Church with dirty jeans and bare feet. All we had there was plain wooden pews and floors. But now our pews are upholstered and we have this beautiful shag carpet. I think we should put a box of rubber sandals in the back of the church and let the kids put them on when they come in."

In keeping with this sentiment, one of the men

made a sign and put it up the following Sunday. The letters were bold and simple, "No bare feet allowed in the church."

It happened that Churck arrived earlier than usual that morning. He saw the sign and took it down. With a great feeling of sadness for this shallow display of priorities, Chuck called a meeting of the board and membership.

"I saw the sign outside," he began, "and took it down. I've called this meeting to see if we can't again evaluate our position as a church. All of you have seen God at work among the drug and hippie culture. The commune ministry is being blessed of the Lord. We now have fifteen houses in southern California alone. And you might be interested to know that Cherise and Jim Manning from the Riverside Miracle House were married recently and have gone to direct a new commune ministry in Oregon.

"I know," continued Chuck, "there is some uptightness about the dirty jeans and bare feet. I'm told some of the kids put their bare feet up on the hymnbook racks and even put their toes up through the communion cup holders. In a sense it is we older established Christians who are on trial before the young people. We are the ones who told them about James 2 and 1 John 2:8. The kind of action we displayed today puts, as James said, a question mark across our faith. When this happens we have to ask ourselves who or what it is that controls and guides our motives."

Chuck paused for a moment, then with jaw set firm and his brown eyes fixed with rock-hard determination said, "If because of our plush carpeting we have to close the door to one young person who has bare feet, then I'm personally in favor of ripping out all the carpeting and having bare concrete floors.

"If because of dirty jeans we have to say to one young person I am sorry you can't come into church tonight, your jeans are too dirty, then I am in favor of getting rid of the upholstered pews. Let's get benches or steel chairs or something we can wash off. But let's not ever, ever, close the door to anyone because of dress or the way he looks."

In the months that followed, the older established membership at Calvary did reevaluate their motives and caught Chuck's vision. Only three members who began with Chuck in the "doll house" left. One was an eighty-year-old man who said, "I am sorry but I am just too old to understand or appreciate the new youth movement." Another was a spinster woman and her mother who lived in Newport and felt the drive to Santa Ana was too long.

This remarkable change in attitude prompted a singing group at Calvary to compose what has almost become a theme song. "Long hairs, short hairs, some coats and ties; people finally coming around, looking past the hair, straight into the eyes—people finally coming around."

And to everyone's amazement the upholstery and carpeting did not wear out. "Partly," said one person, "because the Lord worked in the young people's lives and their jeans became cleaner and cleaner. And it just seemed that God gave special endurance to the carpet and pews. In spite of our tremendous traffic, they just keep looking like new."

The traffic the person referred to, came not from the three hundred people the church was designed to hold, but from the hundreds that crowded into the chapel during the following months. Chuck designed the church to hold three hundred never dreaming it would ever be completely filled. He believed an average attendance of approximately two hundred seventy was an ideal congregation.

"I felt," said Chuck, "that a congregation of this size would give me a tight personal ministry and also give a tremendous base from which to develop a strong missions and home outreach program."

But the first Sunday in June of 1969, when the new Calvary Chapel opened, the ushers scrambled to find chairs to seat the unexpected crowds. "It's just because we're new and this is opening Sunday," said Chuck and some of the membership. "Next Sunday we'll be back to normal."

But on the second Sunday the ushers again ran out of chairs and people sat on the floor. And the third Sunday was a larger, more frantic repeat of the first and second Sunday.

On that third Sunday there wasn't room to stand in the foyer. Some stood outside looking in through the long glass windows.

After five weeks in the new sanctuary, Chuck decided to hold double services. And in two months the ushers were again bringing in extra chairs for the two services.

A year later, Calvary doubled its seating capacity by pushing out the side walls and putting in folding chairs. But this still did not adequately hold all those who wanted to be fed. By mid 1971 Chuck began holding three morning services—8:00, 9:30 and 11:00 A.M. To make sure everyone who came had a seat, the ushers regularly set up five hundred extra chairs on the outside patio.

Chuck's format never varied. Except when he came to the New Testament. There he cut his Bible study survey from ten to five chapters per Sunday. Partly because he wanted to spend more time developing the important truths of the New Testament. And partly to accommodate Calvary member, Ed Plummer, who felt burdened to preserve on hour-long cassette tapes a complete library of Chuck's messages.

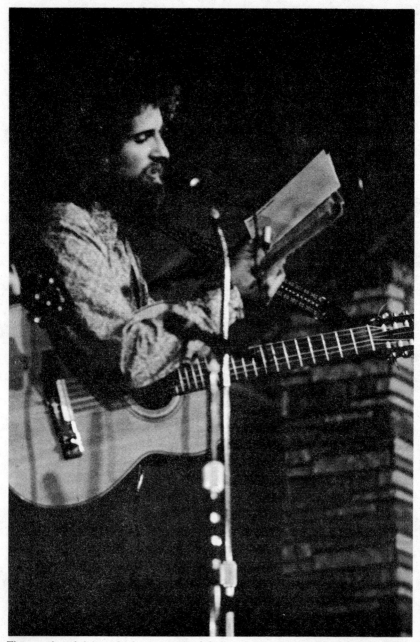
The music ministry which grew out of Calvary was a natural expression of love and praise to Jesus who created new life and love in hundreds of young people.

CHAPTER SEVEN

The Beginning of Ministries

The words, ONE WAY, on the front cover of the catalog are divided by a hand with an extended index finger. JESUS SAID, "LEARN OF ME" is across the top of the page and at the bottom are the words, CALVARY CHAPEL TAPE OUTREACH CATALOG.

Inside is Calvary Chapel's statement of purpose:

The Calvary Chapel Church has been formed as a fellowship of believers in the Lordship of Jesus Christ. Our supreme desire is to know Christ and to be conformed into His image by the power of the Holy Spirit. We are not a denominational church, nor are we opposed to denominations as such, only their overemphasis of the doctrinal differences that have led to the division of the Body of Christ.

We believe that the only true basis of

Christian fellowship is His (*Agape*) love, which is greater than any differences we possess and without which we have no right to claim ourselves Christians.

WE BELIEVE   Worship of God should be Spiritual.

Therefore: We remain flexible and yielded to the leading of the Holy Spirit to direct our worship.

WE BELIEVE   Worship of God should be Inspirational.

Therefore: We give a great place to music in our worship.

WE BELIEVE   Worship of God should be Intelligent.

Therefore: Our services are designed with great emphasis upon teaching the Word of God that He might instruct us how He would be worshiped.

WE BELIEVE   Worship of God is Fruitful.

Therefore: We look for His love in our lives as the supreme manifestation that we have truly been worshiping Him.

It was a strong desire for people to be strengthened, blessed and brought closer to God that prompted Ed Plummer to begin recording Chuck's messages.

"I started to record shortly after we moved to the Greenville property," Ed explained. "First because I wanted to have something meaningful to share with the thirty to thirty-five people who gathered in our home for a weekly Bible study. Then as I saw how practical Chuck's messages were for today's problems and how his instruction from the Word began to affect our lives, I felt burdened to share the tapes with a larger audience."

As marketing manager for a large Pasadena-based electronics firm, Ed had the technical know-how and experience to begin duplicating the tapes. He started with a reel-to-reel seven-inch Sony recorder and four separate cassette decks that produced four tapes at one time. When people in the church heard of Ed's project, they began requesting copies for their friends and relatives.

The demand for tapes grew so rapidly that what started as an extra avocation, in two years became Ed's full-time vocation.

In a bold step of faith in the prime of his career, Ed quit his marketing manager's job and formed Promedia, a small company designed to mass produce and distribute the growing library of Chuck's recorded Bible studies.

"It was a tough decision at first to think about quitting my job," said Ed, "but Chuck taught us that if God is guiding us into a work, He will also provide."

The provision came according to Ed's faith. He soon bought a high-speed duplicator plus a slave unit that would produce eight more tapes. Ed is now able to make twelve tapes in a single six-minute pass.

Ed started Promedia as an independent auxiliary arm of Calvary's outreach program with forty-eight tapes per month. Sales currently run over two thousand with a projection to double this in the next few years. "And," said Ed, "our sales come almost exclusively by word of mouth. Our recently published catalog is the first serious advertising."

Ed finds it exciting to learn where the tapes are going and how they are being used. A man in Kansas City has a fellowship of over three hundred people and uses Chuck's tapes as their primary teaching aid.

Recently a man who had just been released from San Quentin came to Calvary and told Chuck how he had found the Lord through listening to a tape.

In addition to being distributed and used in almost every prison in California, the tapes are going all over the world. There are fifteen Bible study groups in Hawaii who use them and many small groups of servicemen in Vietnam gather around a cassette recorder and listen to Chuck's Bible studies.

"Some of the stories we hear of the tape's effectiveness," said Ed, "are almost unbelievable. A missionary with Wycliffe Bible Translators in Peru wrote and told us of a young man who cycled all the way from Canada to Lima and found the Lord after listening to a tape. The missionary was using this in a group Bible study.

"But one of the cutest stories involving the tape's outreach concerns a woman who had been unable to get her husband out to church in forty years. The husband wouldn't allow his wife to discuss her church life with him. One evening she was in the living room by herself listening to a Bible study tape. Halfway through, she left the room for a moment but forgot to turn off the recorder. When she turned the corner to go down the hall, she ran smack into her her husband. He had been standing in the hallway listening. That little surprise broke the ice of forty years and he is now a regular attender at Calvary."

★   ★   ★

"Worship of God should be Inspirational. We therefore give great place to music in our worship."

When fifteen hundred Sunday evening worshipers raise their hands above their radiant faces and sing, "I will lift up my hands unto the Lord," this second article of Calvary's statement of purpose almost becomes an understatement. And fewer moments are more inspirational than when hundreds of Bibles flip open and the congregation joyously sings Jeremiah 31:12 or the powerful Psalm 150. Or when after a full ninety-minute Bible study the Calvary congregation stands and sings a reverent and thunderous Lord's Prayer.

Most newcomers to Calvary accept the unique congregational singing and Maranatha rock concerts as always being a part of Calvary. But the revolutionary new musical trends didn't occur until early in 1969.

The trends grew slowly at first. They came mostly from the young people's creative urge to find a new combination of sound and words to praise their Lord. When they received these choruses from the Lord, they felt an unquenchable desire to share them with others.

One of those who wanted to share her new faith was Marsha Carter, a fair-haired talented young musician from Claremont. Marsha had repeatedly tried and failed to share her faith with some of her musician friends. Each time she spoke about the Lord, her friends laughed and jokingly brushed aside her words. But Marsha didn't give up. She asked the Lord to give her a song that would best express her feelings and communicate her faith in a meaningful way.

"Hi gang," she said one day to her friends. "I've got a new song. Would you like to hear it?"

"Great!" they said. "Sing on!"

Then in a beautiful soprano voice Marsha sang some words that seemed to her friends to come from a different dimension. The stanzas were beautiful but the chorus hit the small group like thunder.

"And Jesus said, 'Come to the water, stand
   by My side.
I know you are thirsty; you won't be denied.
I felt every teardrop when in darkness you
   cried,
And I strove to remind you that for those tears
   I died.' "

Folk services with Bible study, various music groups and group singing help communicate the real love so many people have searched for all their lives.

There was some lighthearted joking when Marsha first started to sing but no one spoke when she came to the last stanza.

"Jesus, I give You my heart and my soul.
I know that without God, I'd never be whole.
Saviour, You opened all the right doors,
And I thank You and praise You from
    earth's humble shores.
Take me, I'm Yours."

One of the young men who allowed Christ to take him that afternoon was Pete Jacobs, a brilliant musician, who later became the leader for the highly talented Children of the Day singing group.

The Holy Spirit used Marsha's song as an effective tool to win her musician friends to the Lord and also as an inspirational catalyst for other young people to express their inner spiritual feelings. "Come to the Waters" later became the title of a best-selling record album.

One group to respond to the new music and to Calvary's ministry was that of four men who called themselves the Love Song. Two members of the group, Chuck Girard and Tom Coombes, met when they were mustered out of the army together. Both were highly talented musicians and separately had taken drugs. "Because," they said, "we were on a quest for God and the truth of what life was all about."

"At first LSD got me thinking about God," said Chuck Girard. "It completely blew my mind and opened it to things I never knew existed. I didn't know God but thought I could find Him through what I thought was a spiritual experience brought on by drugs. Only trouble was that after a while I was happy only when I took drugs and when I came down I would have long periods of depression."

What was true for Chuck Girard was also true for Tom and their friends who were now living together in Laguna in a kind of drug family.

"We would all share our drug experiences," said Tom, "but it was really the blind leading the blind."

One night after getting into trouble in Las Vegas, Chuck and Tom began to think about the direction of their lives. Right after the trouble in Las Vegas it seemed every second hitchhiker they picked up told them about Calvary Chapel.

"There's something neat happening at Calvary," the hitchhikers would say. Others talked negatively and said, "Don't go up there, man. They're too fanatical!"

Because so many people kept asking Chuck and Tom if they had been to Calvary, they decided to go.

"I really didn't expect to find what I was looking for," said Chuck Girard. "But when I walked inside I knew I had found the love I was searching for all along. In that instant I knew it was real. Deep inside I sensed that what I experienced before was false. But there was nothing false about the love I felt that first night at Calvary.

"When Pastor Smith spoke it just seemed everything he said broke down the intellectual barriers I had built up. Besides I was impressed by the way he looked. Here was a guy who was plainly happy. He was just radiant and humble. Nothing like the sober guru systems I had known. Those guys acted mystical, as if they knew a lot, when they really didn't know a thing.

"But Pastor Smith wasn't at all like that. The words he spoke and the music the people sang were honest and basic. And it cut me right in the heart. I found out that the Word of God really is a two-edged sword. It completely leveled me! For the first time in my life I had to admit I really didn't have it all together and I needed God in my life. That night I committed my life and my music to the Lord."

Tom Coombes came to Calvary the same night and gave his heart to the Lord. But it wasn't until a day later that the full force of what he had done hit him.

"And then," said Tom, "it was as if the last piece of a great puzzle had fallen into place and God showed me how He had been working in my life to bring me to Himself."

"I remember," continued Tom, "that after we got into trouble in Las Vegas for possession of drugs, I met a girl I had known in Salt Lake City. She had been part of the same drug family when I lived there. When I spoke to her, I noticed she was completely different. I mean, man, she was changed! She was just filled with love and when I asked her what happened she said that she was really happy every day since she had known Jesus because He was with her everywhere she went. And then she talked me into coming down to the House of Miracles in Newport Beach. It just so happened everyone was asleep when we got there and I went home. But I remember being impressed with the little stickers on the door, 'Happiness is Jesus,' and 'Peace is Jesus.'"

Tom went on to recall how a few days later he and a few of his friends got into a heated argument about tongues. They had heard about it and wanted to find what this was all about. The only people they knew who might help them were the Christians who lived in the House of Miracles in Newport Beach. They were welcomed and invited to stay for supper.

"I remember how impressed I was with their simple prayer before dinner," said Tom. "They prayed, 'God, thank You for all this food. We just thank You for each other, in Jesus' name.'"

One of the elders at the House of Miracles began very kindly to answer their questions. "First of all," he said, "many people have different and strange ideas about tongues because they don't really read their Bibles. Basically, Chuck Smith has taught us that tongues are great if you use it as praise to God in your own private devotions or very small fellowship. He strongly discourages tongues in public worship and if it is in a small group they must be followed by *true* interpretation. The interpretation is not a message to people in the church but praise to God. Sort of like a psalm. The apostle Paul says, 'He that speaketh in an unknown tongue speaks not unto men, but unto God.'"

The elder continued to talk about Paul not wanting to speak a lot of words in the church that people couldn't understand. By this time, Tom had

75

difficulty understanding everything the elder was saying. The elder sensed this, paused and asked Tom if he was born again.

"Yeah," said Tom, "I think so."

Since it was Sunday night the elder suggested they go to Calvary Chapel and listen to a Bible study. "And," said Tom, "the way he said it amazed me because I could see he and the others at the House were really excited about going to church."

When Tom walked inside the Chapel he was completely overwhelmed with the large crowd of happy people waiting for the service to begin. "But what really blew my mind," said Tom, "was Chuck Smith. I sat about four rows from the front and watched him closely. And, wow! All he did was speak to us like he was talking to a single person. All the time he had a big smile on his face. Even when he said words like someday the world's going to come to an end!"

That night Chuck, Tom and some of their friends stayed behind and waited until everyone left. Chuck Girard wanted to tell Chuck Smith what had happened in his heart. Tom did too. But not as much as Chuck. He was thinking about what was going to happen the following morning. Tom and his friends were scheduled to appear in court for sentencing on a drug possession charge. They told Chuck Smith about it and he prayed for them.

The next morning the fellows appeared in court, frightened, but not like they had been a few days before. When the judge passed out the sentence, Tom said, "I felt a keen sense of justice being done and I knew the Lord had worked a miracle. Our sentence was for one of the fellows, who's no longer with us, to go to jail for fifteen weekends. And the judge worked it out so it could be on Mondays and Tuesdays. This was so we could begin to minister with our music on Saturdays and Sundays."

Tom knew God was in all of this and right then and there committed his life and music to Him.

Letters encourage the staff at Maranatha where the profit is seeing God work through the tapes, free concerts, records, posters, brochures and tracts.

CHAPTER EIGHT

Maranatha!

"I'm not a rock festival fan. I'm a conservative missionary pilot from Rhodesia. But I've been concerned for churches and Christians to come back to a biblical concept of what Christianity is all about. I believe the Jesus Movement with their music and witnessing, their ability to look past outside appearances, and the emphasis on the Word is a beautiful expression of what the true gospel is all about.

"I repeat, I am not a rock fan. I don't understand it all. But I was thrilled with the love, concern, tenderness and spontaneity these kids displayed at a concert I attended in the Long Beach Municipal Auditorium."

There were and are many like this missionary who find the new approach to music difficult to understand and digest. But the music is composed and played for the youth of the seventies. And for every adult who can't understand, there are thousands of the youth who do.

"And," said Bob Wall, current lead guitarist for the Love Song, "we want to reach the kids who listen to Led Zeppelin and the Rolling Stones. They offer a beat. But we have a message given to us by God and it's all about His Son Jesus Christ."

"Bob is right," said Chuck Smith. "The Love Song does have a message. After they accepted the Lord and began sharing their talents in the Chapel and special concerts, the Lord gave them fantastic new songs. This immediately opened up a whole new dimension at Calvary. In a sense we became all things to all men in order to win them. Kids started coming in tremendous numbers just to hear the music. Whenever they take part in the service or hold concerts, the young musicians always give their personal testimonies and an opportunity for people to accept Christ."

Love Song not only attracted large groups of young people to come and listen to their music. They inspired other talented groups to form and begin using their talents for Jesus.

Love Song signed with United Artists specifically to get their music and message out on a national level. Groups like Country Faith, Blessed Hope, along with Love Song and others hold concerts in high schools, the Long Beach auditorium and Calvary Chapel, in addition to national and international tours. Love Song, Blessed Hope and other groups and vocalists combined their talents to produce "The Everlasting Living Jesus Concert" album. This was quickly followed by the talented Children of the Day's album, "Come to the Waters." Response to the two albums was a staggering twenty-five thousand copies sold during the first six months of their release.

To handle the runaway record sales, concert bookings, voluminous follow-up mail and Bible correspondence courses, Calvary formed a subsidiary nonprofit organization called Maranatha Music/Publishing.

Belying the horror of five dark years on drugs and seventeen months of psychotherapy, handsome Mike McIntosh capably handles the Maranatha business. "We have thirty counselors," he says matter-of-factly, "marking and sending out the Navigator Bible correspondence course."

Each person who makes a profession of faith at a concert or at Calvary receives lesson one of a fourteen-lesson course. When the new convert returns lesson one, lesson two is sent. This seems to be the easiest and most effective method to handle the ten to fifteen thousand yearly decisions and get them into a systematic study of the Word.

"I was a car salesman before I came to Christ," said Mike. "All I thought about was how to make a sale and a fat profit for myself. But here in Maranatha, thanks to Jesus, we're more interested in ministering to people. All the money we do make on sales goes to cover our concert expenses. Our concerts are always free. We also keep the cost of the tapes Ed Plummer produces for us down to a bare minimum.

"At Maranatha we believe the most exciting profit

for us is seeing God at work through the tapes, music and our illustrations."

A letter from England reflects the influence of the Maranatha outreach:

"I've just attended a concert given by Country Faith in All Saints Church, Woodford Greens, Essex. The atmosphere was wonderful and everybody enjoyed it. A credit to the group. It was wonderful to share in their love and knowledge of Jesus Christ. It was also a pleasure to hear someone singing the name of the Lord with such love and meaning. What a change from today's songs that hold no meaning to life. The group told us of an album showing a red dove on the cover. Would you please send me a copy."

Another letter from an Episcopal priest in Florida reads:

"Praise the Lord! I have your record on loan from a friend. How do I get more? Please send me four copies. I'm an Episcopal clergyman whom the Lord turned on a few years ago. And I'm more excited about your music as a vehicle for the Lord's outreach than almost anything I've heard. Is the music published? Can I get copies for use in worship and prayer groups?

Yours in Christ . . ."

The Maranatha staff praises the Lord for the growing tape and music outreach and also for the unusual graphic arts ministry. When Maranatha incorporated in December 1971, Mike, Chuck and others almost overlooked the word "Publications" in their official registration. They were thinking only of their music and momentarily forgot the significance of their graphic arts ministry.

"Why, I'll never know," said Mike, "because Kernie Erickson, Greg Laurie and others who are involved in designing record jackets, posters, bumper stickers, tracts and other graphic arts materials, are an integral part of Calvary's outreach."

Soft spoken, with dancing blue eyes, balding and wearing a full beard, Kernie looks the part of an Old World artist, except that he is very much a part of today's world.

For years Kernie had looked for a way to express his inner feelings and had tried to find God through drugs. The night he found Christ at Calvary, Kernie knew his search was ended and also knew he wanted to share God's eternal message through his art.

At first he didn't know how he was going to do it and became frustrated that he had wasted so many years of his life.

"But then as I began to pray and read the Scriptures," said Kernie, "the Lord seemed to say, 'I can use your whole past for my glory but you must be willing to keep your eyes on Me. When you do, I will give you the desires of your heart.'

"It took six months of struggling to do it my way," continued Kernie, "before I said, 'OK, Lord. If You want me to draw for You, fine. I am no longer going to struggle to find an avenue of service. Please take over.'"

About a week after Kernie prayed, he ran into

Dempster Evans at a beach baptism. They talked and Dempster said, "Yes, as a matter of fact I do need help. I've been looking for someone to help me."

"Dempster told me about Maranatha," said Kernie. "It was just getting started. God brought it all together. Now I'm on my own with Greg and another fellow and we're praising the Lord through our art work."

"Here's a poster I'm doing for Wycliffe Bible Translators," continued Kernie. "We call it, 'Wow.' It's designed with the idea of making Wycliffe known to college students as a possible avenue of service. I like doing posters like this because it's hand done and satisfies my artistic and aesthetic interest. But more importantly, the major part of the poster is Scripture."

Kernie believes that lifting up the name of the Lord is the secret for success in Christian service. This, he says, is what sells bumper stickers, record albums, and will move people to respond to Wycliffe's desire of reaching 160 million people who need the Word of God in their own language.

Greg Laurie, Kernie's youthful partner, knows from personal experience that this is dramatically true. His first eight-page cartoon tract, *Living Water*, has exceeded 300,000 copies.

Like Kernie, the Love Song and others, Greg experimented with drugs. But not because he was searching for God. Greg's drug taking was an attempt to escape the hollow madness that surrounded his life and that of his seven-time divorced mother.

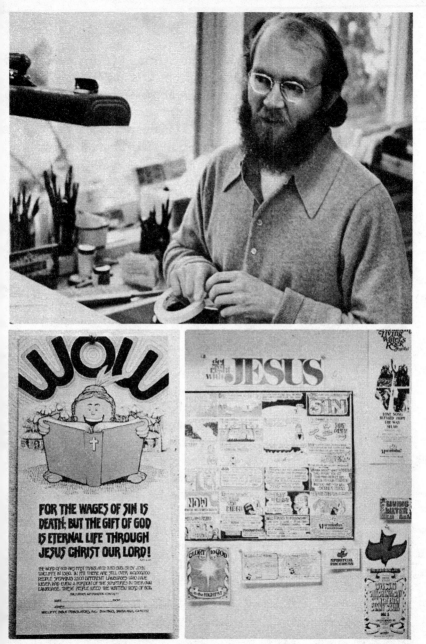

Multiple ministries under the leadership and guidance of Maranatha are designed to relate to youth who are looking for God but don't know where to find Him.

At nineteen, soft-spoken Greg Laurie wears shoulder-length hair, a full beard, and exudes a quiet beautiful Christian character. The kind that is normally displayed after years of obedience and conformity to Christ. Greg's character development becomes all the more incredible when he shares his testimony.

"My mother was married and divorced seven times," he said. "And about all I can remember about my pre- and early teens is the bitter hatred of arguing parents or the folly of promiscuous adults trying to drink their way to happiness.

"In my late teens I rebelled and decided I didn't want anything to do with the phony adult world. I tried to find some answers by getting drunk with the gang, becoming a football player and going out with girls. But after a while I realized I wasn't any different than my mother.

"Then I thought the hippies might have an answer and I began using marijuana. Not really heavy, but just enough for me to realize I was coming up empty inside and didn't know what to do about it.

"During a lunch break in high school I decided to buy some acid. But before I got to buy it I ran into a group of kids singing songs. It sounded neat and I went over to find out what their thing was. Here were all these kids radiating a joy that I couldn't pinpoint. So I sat off to one side and listened. All they sang about was Jesus. Suddenly a little bearded guy gets up and tells us his name is Lonnie Frisbee and starts right in preaching from the Bible. It wasn't watered down or jazzed up to try and appeal to the kids. Just right out of the Word.

"He said that if you're not for Jesus you're against Him—one or the other! We would have to choose what we individually would do with Christ. This really hit me because it had never been put to me this way before. Then things started to spark and burn inside. All of a sudden I realized I believed in God but had cluttered Him up with so many other things.

"I had a great desire to have this salvation Lonnie said anyone could have by accepting Christ as his personal Saviour. When Lonnie gave an invitation to accept Jesus, I wanted to go up but stopped when I saw some of my old friends standing in the crowd. But then something seemed to grab and pick me up. Before I knew it I was up front praying and accepted Jesus into my life.

"The second I started to pray I remember it felt like something was lifted off my back and all the sins I had ever committed were gone. I was free! It was just great! People came up and hugged me and told me how wonderful it was to know Jesus.

"I had accepted Christ but no one told me it was wrong to take drugs. That afternoon I went out to the mountains with my weed and pipe. As I sat there smoking away and looking all around at the beauty of the trees, sky and mountains and listening to the birds, something inside seemed to say, 'You don't need this anymore. I've got something new for you.' Immediately I threw out the weed, broke my pipe and turned down drugs from that moment on. And with this desire gone came the desire to read the Bible, pray and attend church. I also felt a keen desire to witness.

"I was a week old in the Lord and the only tract I had didn't seem to relate to the young people I was talking to."

Chuck Smith remembers when Greg first came to Calvary. He introduced himself and told Chuck he had just accepted the Lord a few weeks before and had given his talent to the Lord. Chuck thought he was finished speaking, smiled and said, "That's glorious! Praise the Lord!"

But Greg just kept right on talking and said, "The other day in art class the teacher gave us an assignment to do a cartoon. I've always wanted to be a cartoonist and since coming to the Lord I especially wanted to express in art something of how I feel about Jesus. When I got this assignment I picked up a wide piece of paper, my felt pen, and prayed asking the Lord to give me an idea. In a half hour I had this."

Greg showed Chuck twenty-two frames of cartoon drawings illustrating God's provision and plan of salvation for man. "I am calling this, *Living Water*," Greg said. "I got the idea from Scriptures you used in a message from the Gospel of John where Jesus said, 'He who drinks of the water that I give shall have rivers of living water flowing out from his innermost being.'"

"I was so impressed with what Greg showed me," said Chuck, "I thought anything this clever should be published. I had a printer make up 5,000 copies. They were gone in a week. I returned to the printer a second time and had 20,000 made up. They also were gone in a week! The third time I ordered 100,000 copies and in a little over a year's time, we doubled our order to 200,000 more."

Greg has since produced a tract he calls, "Spiritual Progress," which is also cartoon characters showing new Christians how to live their new lives guided by the Holy Spirit.

"This," says Greg with a tongue-in-cheek smile, "is for us oldies, a year or so old in the Lord."

Late in November 1971, thinking they had missed that year's Christmas trade but going ahead in faith, Kernie and Greg produced three contemporary design Christmas cards. To their surprise they sold out the 25,000 cards that were printed.

Greg, like Kernie, believes the work itself is its own reward. But sometimes the Lord allows them to hear how their art has helped someone.

Greg pulled open a drawer in his desk and took out a dirty, dog-eared copy of his little three by five inch *Living Water* tract and an equally battered letter. It was a letter he had received a short time ago from San Quentin Prison and read:

> "A while ago I was given a little booklet entitled 'Living Water'. I read it and thought it was good but put it away with some letters and forgot about it. Then one day I found it again and started to read it. As I read I felt God was talking to me and I began to understand that I needed Him and I should follow Him. Now I am sending this booklet back to you with the hope that you will give it to someone who hasn't quite found his way back to Christ yet."

"And," said Greg thoughtfully, "that's exactly what I am going to do."

At a water baptismal service Chuck Smith says, "As you come up out of the water, remember, you come up in newness of life. You are new creatures in Christ Jesus."

CHAPTER NINE

Hold Me Down a Long Time

If you could blot out the old Gillette mansion across the bay or close your eyes to luxury craft plying out to sea, the cove could be straight out of *Treasure Island*. It's the kind of place buccaneers would choose to put ashore in their longboats and under the silent gaze of the overhanging pockmarked cliffs, bury their ill-gotten treasure.

Today, Pirate's Cove is part of southern California's Corona del Mar beach and the only longboats and buccaneers who put into this cove are in the imaginations of the hundreds of children who scramble over its sand colored cliffs.

But there are burials in this sheltered cove. They're called water baptisms. On these occasions, Chuck Smith and three assistants slowly, deliberately and reverently immerse hundreds of young men and women into the cool salt water.

There are those who are confused about Calvary's water baptisms. Some believe them to be cultish. Others can't believe people do things like this anymore. But for the many who have been baptized, there is nothing cultish about obeying and rejoicing in the promises and instruction of Romans, chapter six. Nor does it matter to them what people think. The Lord Himself was baptized and His example is all the instruction the young people at Calvary need to obey Him.

During one of Calvary's beach baptisms hundreds of onlookers, families and friends of those being baptized covered the surrounding cliffs of Pirate's Cove. There were beards, bare feet, sandals, tank tops, shorts, cut-offs, shirts and ties, long dresses, long hair and short. The morning was crisp and clean, the sky rich blue and, except for the occasional low moan of a distant fog horn, the scene was a Galilean hillside.

There was a relaxed mood of reverence and expectancy. People laughed and talked together good naturedly. But there was no loud noise or shouting. Even the children who made sand castles or played tag on the beach were quiet and respectful.

Just before the baptism, Chuck called together those being baptized. Dressed in a white short sleeve turtle-neck T-shirt and gray slacks, Chuck stood barefoot in the refreshingly cool 68 degree water a few feet off shore. With the gentle lapping of waves around his feet and the occasional cry of a herring gull overhead, Chuck spoke.

"Before coming to Christ," he said, "we used to live our lives in the flesh. But now that old life is dead and we are about to symbolically bury all the remnants of the past. When Jesus was baptized the heavens were opened and the Spirit of God descended on Him like a dove. Today, in this beautiful baptismal experience, each one of you can, in faith, receive the strength of God's Holy Spirit to live your life each day in ways that will bring honor and glory to our Lord. As you come up out of the water, remember you come up in newness of life. You are new creatures in Christ Jesus.

"Secondly," continued Chuck, "expect the enemy to attack. The Bible says that immediately after Jesus was baptized, He was led by the Spirit into the wilderness and tempted by the devil. Each time you have a great spiritual experience, Satan will try to defeat and rob you of the blessing God has given. But if you're prepared to claim the spiritual victory Christ has already won for you, you don't have to worry. The Bible says that if we draw near to God, God draws near to us, which means automatically the devil flees from us. But the fight won't be easy. Satan will subtly try to prove that your life isn't new. He'll bring up the old desires and temptations of the flesh. But I repeat, resist the devil, draw near to God and claim the victory of new life in Christ. Let's pray.

"Lord bless this gathering. Let this be a rich, beautiful and meaningful day as we identify ourselves with Jesus Christ. Bless each one who takes this step of faith and let the power of the Holy Spirit descend and minister to us. Let it be a time of glorious rejoicing and praise to Jesus Christ. We ask it in His name. Amen."

Chuck then told them to remain on the shore

until he and his assistants came to get them. Slowly, carefully, with arms intertwined or clasped across each one's shoulders or around his waist, Chuck led the person being baptized into the water. Turning their backs from the crowd, he lingered and talked with each one before the actual act of baptism. As they walked out into the water Chuck said, "This is the end of the road for the old life. You have come now to bury it. For if any man be in Christ Jesus he is a new creature. The old things are passed away and all things have become new. From now on it's going to be a new kind of life with Jesus Christ at the controls. He is the Lord of our lives and wants to control and give us the power to live this new life."

Chuck's voice was calm, reassuring, possessing a rare quality of kindness and strength. When they were waist deep, Chuck positioned his strong arm around the person's shoulder to place them beneath the water and said, "Because you have accepted Jesus Christ as your Saviour and want Him to be the Lord of your life, I baptize you in the Name of the Father, and the Son, and the Holy Spirit."

An instant before each person felt the waters close over his head in symbolic death to his old life, he heard, "This is it. The old is buried!" And as he came up out of the water Chuck said, "This is the beginning of the new. Let's walk with Jesus!"

In every case the emotion of the moment exploded and infected the onlookers. Those who waited on the shore raised their hands. Some with eyes closed sang the beautiful "I will lift up my hands unto the Lord."

94

The baptism of each person is different and beautiful in its own way. For on-lookers and those baptized, it is a never-to-be-forgotten spiritual experience.

As person after person joyously walked back to shore, they fell into the warm embraces of friends and loved ones who waited to weep with the tears of unusual joy and gladness. Many onlookers with no emotional ties to Calvary felt the overwhelming power of the Holy Spirit and found themselves wiping tears from their cheeks.

Susan Cato, the vivacious young housewife of a Santa Ana restauranteur, spent part of the morning interviewing some of those to be baptized. She asked one young man why he wanted to be baptized. "Mostly," he said, "to let God know that I really want to serve Him."

One girl told Susan she was in the August baptism and because of the wall-to-wall people, stood waist deep for three hours before her turn came up. "It got a little windy and chilly," she said, "but no one cared because the Spirit in the crowd was something that had to be felt to be understood."

"As I turned to watch some of those who were being baptized," said Susan, "I began to feel something of the Spirit the girl had talked about. Just overwhelmingly warm and content, like I had always been a part of Calvary. I brushed away the tears that started to flow and thought what a strange way for a Presbyterian to act. But I didn't care. It was one of the most moving experiences of my life!"

For onlookers and those being baptized that October, it was indeed a never-to-be-forgotten spiritual experience.

"Each baptism is uniquely different and beautiful in its own way," said Chuck later. "But there is one baptism I remember above all others. I had been teaching in our Bible class that baptism represents a burial, a positive break with the past. Because many of our people have lived sordid lives they feel this emphasis is important. I never knew how important until I came to baptize one young man. As we walked out into the water he said with tears in his eyes, 'Hold me down a long time, Chuck. I've got a lot to bury.' "

Time, Reader's Digest, Look and other magazines and papers from around the world have reported what is happening at Calvary. They see it. Some like Look photographers, Jack and Betty Cheetham, feel it and respond to the Person who is making it happen. But most don't really see because they look without spiritual understanding.

Among the many things they can't understand is why week after week more and more people respond to God. Why during the past two years more than twenty thousand accepted Christ and over eight thousand were baptized at Corona del Mar. And why the Jesus Movement hasn't died.

Ken Gulliksen, the blond and good looking assistant pastor at Calvary, answers these questions by saying, "If you're racing down a highway on your chopper and run out of gas you'll come to a stop no matter how powerful and menacing you appear. But the Jesus Movement will never run out of gas because God started it and He is without beginning or end. He is beyond the vanishing point and therefore the source of all energy. And the energy we run on is not gas, unrest or hate. It's pure peace and *agape* love!"

Ken further explains that the Jesus Movement

didn't happen because theologians tried to work up a new form of worship. Or because a bunch of long-haired kids began beating people over the heads with Bibles. It happened because God wanted it to happen in His time schedule. And the people at Calvary are having the glorious privilege of participating in His plan.

Some people date the movement as beginning in 1961 when small groups began to respond to the tug of God's Holy Spirit. Others say it was in the early fifties. "This is not an isolated happening in these last days," Ken said. "In Genesis we read, 'In the beginning God created the heaven and the earth . . . and the Spirit of God moved upon the face of the water.' The Jesus Movement started when God's Spirit began to move upon the earth and has continued on throughout history up to the present hour. Many patriarchs down through the centuries, including the present-day servants of Jesus Christ throughout the world, are all part of the Jesus Movement. All fit into God's eternal plan to uplift Jesus and bring men back to God."

People often ask how they can have a Jesus Movement in their church or in their lives. "You can't," said Ken, "because it already is. What you can do is position yourself in the flow of God's Spirit. Coming into the flow is not attending Calvary Chapel or any other church, getting religion or getting in on the Jesus Movement. You can look at the Movement and completely miss Jesus. The Jesus Movement is Jesus Christ moving in your life drawing you into an intimate love relationship with Himself.

"The reason we have so much love at Calvary is because we have been forgiven and we're experiencing the fruit of forgiveness which is love. And those who have been forgiven much, love much."

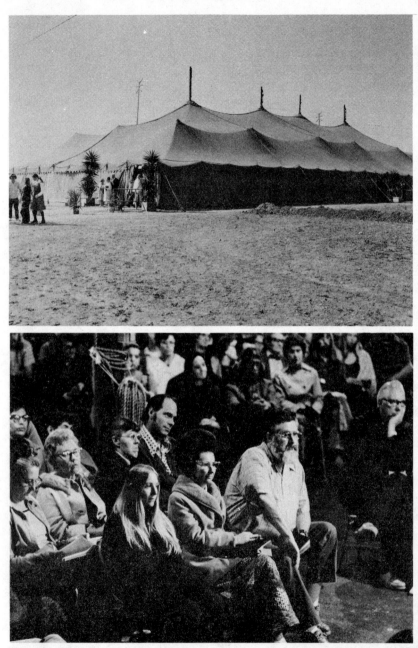
With the rainy season approaching, a tent was the answer to prayer for still growing numbers of people drawn to the Bible studies and worship services.

CHAPTER TEN

Your Servant

November, December and January are months
when people in snowbound climates look longingly
at southern California's vacation ads. Frequently
they show golden-haired girls lounging beside an
emerald swimming pool. Or a shirt-sleeved golfer
driving a ball down a bright green fairway. But the
ad writers didn't have the coastal areas of Costa
Mesa and Newport Beach in mind. Often these are
the coldest and rainiest months of the year here.

Chuck and the Calvary board knew this and were
concerned with the comfort of the more than five
hundred people who were forced Sunday after Sunday to sit outside in the patio.

For months a new and larger church facility was
a foregone conclusion. As the board looked for land
to build, others began looking for a larger meeting
hall to rent.

One day, Ed Riddle, realtor from Calvary, told Chuck about an option he had on eleven acres one block from Calvary Church. Chuck thought the land was great but didn't feel the church needed eleven acres. Nor did they have the $374,000 asking price.

"We were looking for five to seven acres," said Chuck, "but when we looked into the price, we found it would cost almost as much as the eleven acres."

When it became know that Calvary was seriously thinking about buying the eleven acres, a member of Calvary offered his services. "I think I can get the land for $300,000," he said optimistically.

"I don't know," said Chuck. "All the property we've checked out runs from forty to fifty thousand per acre. But go ahead and see what you can do."

Several days later the man returned and said, "I offered the woman who owns the property $300,000 cash. She just happened to need the money and accepted the offer!"

The Calvary board was almost staggered by the unbelievable event. To make up the cash payment, they borrowed $150,000.

The Calvary membership was overjoyed with the obvious hand of the Lord upon their business dealings. All except Chuck. It wasn't that he was unhappy with the property. He was unhappy with the $150,000 note.

One afternoon, before the first interest payment was due, Chuck drove past the new property and thanked the Lord for His unusual provision for Calvary's needs. "Lord," said Chuck, "I don't like to spend Your money unwisely. I think giving it to a savings and loan company for interest is unwise. Would You please do something about this interest note?"

"Hi, honey," said Kay cheerily when Chuck came home. "Ed Riddle called and wants you to call him back. Something about Shell Oil Company wanting to buy 180 by 185 feet of the new property. They want it for a gas station and offered us $150,000!"

With almost eleven acres of prime unencumbered land at their disposal, Chuck and the board decided the quickest way to get everyone under one roof until they could build was to erect a tent.

It was a cold forty degree wet and windy Wednesday night in late November 1971. The Costa Mesa fire marshal had not yet decided what heating equipment he would allow for the big 90 by 180 foot tent. But for fifteen hundred people who gathered for Calvary's third mid-week service, it didn't seem important that the temperature outside almost equalled that on the inside. Many snuggled comfortably in blankets and found an inner warmth from the rich singing, sparkling testimonies of the high schoolers and finally from Chuck's practical study.

When Chuck finished speaking, he prayed specifically for those who were still living an empty, frustrating life outside of Christ. He then asked those who seriously intended to walk with Jesus to stand up. Thirty did!

He asked the thirty to meet with him by the platform for a few minutes, then dismissed the meeting.

"Now," said Chuck, "I want those of you who

have accepted Jesus Christ to know that this is the most glorious thing that has ever happened to you."

At first Chuck's voice reflected the exhaustion of his ninety-minute Bible study. But as he spoke and began wrapping the new believers in their spiritual swaddling clothes, Chuck became visibly refreshed and exhilarated.

"Each one of you," continued Chuck, "will find, for the first time, a beginning consciousness of God's love and fellowship. With this comes the promise that God will begin a special work in your life that will never end.

"Before you go home I want to share three important commands from Scripture. In Matthew 11:28 Jesus says, 'Come unto me all ye that are heavy laden and I will give you rest.' Check that command off! You have shown by your actions that you have indeed come to Christ. You have done your part, now it's God's turn to make His move. I guarantee you on the authority of God's Word that He will give as He promised, a peace and rest you never dreamed existed.

"As you enter into fellowship with God, it's going to be absolutely beautiful. Just think—no more war! You are no longer fighting. No more striving. It's all over. You belong to God! As you go to sleep tonight you're going to say, 'Wow! Am I going to be here in the morning? Is it real?' It is!"

Chuck explained that the second command was found in the first part of verse 29 of Matthew 11 which says, "Take my yoke upon you." He pointed out that the yoke, in addition to being used by oxen to pull a plow, was used to guide the animals.

"What Jesus is saying," said Chuck, "is that he has a work for you to do and wants to guide your life. Before you had your own yoke. You did what you wanted to do. You went where you wanted to go. You did your own thing and bore the backbreaking pressure of life alone. Now the Lord says, "My yoke is easy, My burden is light.'

"When you wake up tomorrow say, 'Okay, Lord! My life is Yours. What do You want me to do? Just whatever You have in mind is okay with me. I am open and want Your will for my life today!"

Chuck briefly illustrated how God sometimes guides in our lives without us being aware it was divine guidance. He told of being in a hospital, praying for a lady who had been in a car accident. As he started to leave, a girl across the room called to him and said, "Hi, Chuck, I go to Calvary Chapel too."

When Chuck asked why she was there she said, "I broke my nose in an accident and am having surgery tomorrow. I'm really scared. Would you pray for me?" Chuck shared some of God's promises and prayed.

"Praise the Lord!" said the girl. "I'm not scared anymore. I know God's going to be with me. Oh, wow! Thank you so much!"

Chuck told the new believers how very excited and happy he was that the Lord led him to this girl. As he went down the hall he prayed, "God, You're so beautiful. There are over three hundred rooms in this hospital and You put that girl in the same room as the other woman. Thank You for the opportunity to minister to her at the same time. That's so glorious, Lord. Just beautiful planning."

Chuck went on to explain how he got in the elevator and pushed the button for the main floor. But when he stepped out, he discovered he was in a nurse's station.

"As I looked around wondering where I was," said Chuck, "I thought I must have pushed the wrong button. But when I stepped into the elevator, I noticed the light said I was on the ground floor. For a moment I just stood looking puzzled. Then a nurse told me that if I was looking for the lobby I wouldn't find it. I had taken the service elevator! She told me I could reach the lobby by walking down a long corridor and turning right at the first corner."

He made the turn and noticed a young girl standing in a doorway crying. As he came closer, the girl looked up. "Oh, Chuck Smith! Praise the Lord!" Chuck recognized her as a Calvary member and asked her why she was crying.

"Oh, I'm so low," she said. "My dearest friend is having brain surgery and the doctors don't think she'll pull through. I was just telling the Lord that I didn't know what to do and asked Him to please send someone to pray with me. When I looked up, you came walking down the hall!"

Chuck said that as he shared the Word and prayed with her, God seemed to tell him that everything was going to be all right and that the girl in surgery would pull through. And the girl, with tears of joy on her face, praised God for sending him.

"Then," said Chuck, "it hit me! Wrong elevator? Stupid mistake? No! I didn't pay attention to the el-

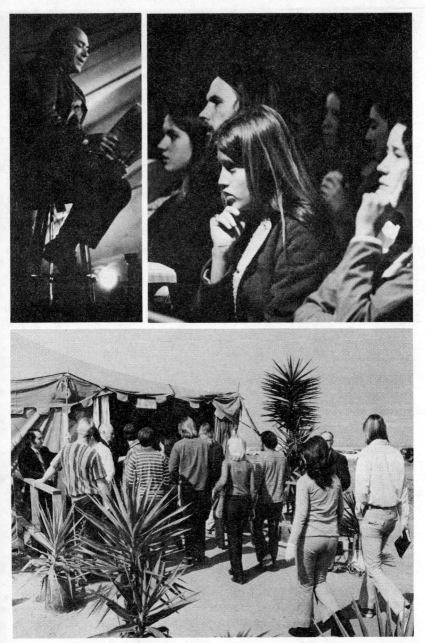

Learning, growing and serving are a part of each person's Christian life, whether he is a newborn lamb, a Bible study leader or the church's senior pastor.

evator upstairs because I was exploding with God's love and blessing. He wanted me to go down that corridor! What a thrill to know that God had His hand in it all the time."

Chuck wrapped up his instruction by giving them the third command found in the last part of verse 29 where Jesus says, "Learn of Me."

With the intenseness of a father giving last minute instructions to a son, Chuck said, "Learning about Jesus is absolutely vital to a newborn Christian. It is the food for your spiritual growth. When you bring a new baby home, you just don't keep going over to the crib and saying, 'Oh, what a beautiful baby' and never bother to feed it.

"That's what each of you are tonight. New babes in Christ and you're all beautiful. But now you've got to be fed and grow strong. It's for this reason we want to give you a New Testament and get you started in a short Bible correspondence course.

"Now," said Chuck, "will you pray out loud and repeat after me.

'Dear God, I come to You tonight in the name of Jesus Christ. I ask You to forgive my sin. Help me to be the kind of person You want me to be. I accept Jesus Christ as my Saviour and as my Lord. Take me over, Lord. Begin to guide and direct my life according to Your will. In Jesus' name I ask it. Amen.'"

There were still clusters of people in the tent, some talking, some singing. But for a moment they were lost to the thirty new believers. Momentarily suspended in time, the realization of what they had done began to dawn in their minds.

108

"Listen," said Chuck with a bright smile, "do you know that God has absolutely nothing against you tonight? Before, sin kept getting in the way, blocking your fellowship with God. But now all the sins you ever committed have been blotted out. God looks at you right now and sees nothing but absolute purity because He sees you in the righteousness of His Son, Jesus Christ.

"One final thing. You've picked up a fringe benefit. I am here to serve you. If you need help, or need someone to talk to or pray with, I am here. The Scriptures say whoever is the minister among you let him be the servant of all. And that's exactly what I am—your servant."

Publisher's Epilogue

Testimonies from His people at Calvary Chapel

(Based on taped interviews by the publishers)

People who love Jesus are drawn together—some sit on chairs and some on the floor—some are joyful and some serious. But all of His people share His love.

Harold

My father was a minister and I grew up in a Christian home. I became a Christian at the age of accountability, maybe the age of six or seven. After my wife and I were married, I kind of rebelled against the church. I had seen too many emotional experiences with no reality.

Then a former pastor of ours began holding services in a trailer court in the area, so we attended the second service they had. And we kept going and the services got a little larger. We rented a Girl Scout building in Costa Mesa and at that time I was asked to be a charter board member. The name Calvary Chapel was chosen at that time.

We tried very hard to do things by our own efforts, without asking the Lord. There were a lot of problems. My wife and I kept talking about leaving. I kept thinking, "Why don't I leave this place?" And this went on for months. I walked out of board meetings, and I didn't know why I stayed on! Then the pastor took a leave of absence and we started getting in guest speakers. One day a board member said, "You know we should get this fellow by the name of Chuck Smith down here."

When Chuck did come and give a message I thought, "Wow, I've never been fed like this." And it wasn't an emotional high. It was something I could think about and remember when I went to work the next week. He spoke straight from the Scripture.

You can probably guess what my feeling as a police officer was when the Jesus Movement hit Calvary Chapel. My first contact was with a couple of long hairs who came to our home where we had Bible studies going. My first thought was to go clean out my medicine cabinet. But we found out these kids were very receptive to the Word. Then they came to the church and walked right up close to the front. It didn't take long to realize these people were really hungry and searching, and also had a lot to give to us. It made me think about people Jesus was most interested in when He was walking on earth—not the upright Pharisee, but the people who needed Him, the harlot and the dirty tax collector who cheated everybody. It made me think, who in the world do I think I am. I sure don't want to be in the category of the Pharisee. These are certainly the people He would help today. So I took a real quick change of mind.

I had accepted Christ, but had never committed my everyday life to Him. I'd had some Christians tell me I couldn't be a Christian and be a policeman. This bothered me because my job was important to me and was the support of my family.

I had worn contact lenses for about eight years. My vision was a little bad so I went to an optometrist for a prescription change. He discovered something wrong with my eyes and sent me to an ophthalmologist who told me I had an eye disease that was going to take my eyesight. This concerned me because I needed good vision on the job.

One Sunday after the service we were going to have a laying on of hands for the sick. My wife said, "Why don't we stay." We usually did stay. Finally I said, "Okay," and we sat in the back of the church. I sat there thinking I'm not going to have hands laid on me. A young fellow got up and said, "I want to accept Christ." I thought, if my wife asks me to go up and get prayed for before they are through talking with this fellow, I'll go. I was sure that would never happen. But no sooner had I thought that than she leaned over and said, "Hey, why don't you go up and get prayed for." I was kind of upset. But I went up and when they laid hands on me, everything just lifted. I had peace I'd never realized before. It was fantastic. When they were praying for me there was a prophecy that if I remained true and committed to the Lord, my love for Him would be known throughout the community.

I'd been told that after cornea transplant operations I could never be a policeman again. So I left my job knowing the Lord would take care of us. I had committed my life to Him. Six months after surgery on the left eye, I was able to come back to work and later discovered I could wear a contact lens on that eye, which I wasn't supposed to be able to do. After six months back on the job I went for the second surgery. Everything was fine. My job was held for me and I walked right back into my office. I knew that was where the Lord wanted me.

Once a year there is a policeman of the year chosen. I was nominated. This was unusual because of my rank, because I'd been out most of the year and because I had not done anything outstanding that I could see. Two weeks later the announcement was made that I was chosen. I had prayed that I would receive this only if the Lord would be glorified. When the announcement came out in the paper the article reported that I keep on my stand the vehicle code and the Holy Bible and that I live by both. The paper said I had been chosen because of my life in Christ. So the prophecy came true—right on the front page of the newspaper. I hadn't told the newsmen any of this. All the information about me came from the department.

I go to the Word, I rely on it and I live it. I only want to be where the Lord wants me.

We really started relying on the Lord at the time of my eye disease. Since then we've had our most fantastic years of marriage. I had never taken hold of my wife's hand and prayed about a problem. Now we'll sit and hold each other's hands and pray about everything together. I would say we really didn't have a happy married life until we got into the Word. The last four to five years have been really fantastic!

Rob

We got married and it was a real bummer. I was
trying to make it in the world. I wasn't happy being
married. I didn't like the responsibility of having to
go to work every day, holding a job. Arnel was
pregnant. We knew a baby was coming. Pressures
were building up and I didn't think I could handle
them. I wanted to get out of it all so badly. But
deep inside I knew that I couldn't leave, 'cause we
were married.

One day I was driving along and I picked up this
guy in Laguna Beach. He was a longhair. He
jumped into the car and he was so happy, so excited, I just figured he had to be stoned. I asked him if
he had any drugs. He said he didn't get stoned on
drugs any more. He had a Bible in his hand and he
shared how the Lord had delivered him. He gave
me a little tract.

He didn't push anything on me. He just said,
"God loves you." Then he got out of the car. But I
felt he hadn't told me enough!

I came home and told Arnel I was going to be a
Christian and it blew her mind. I threw away my
cigarettes and my dope. I tried to be what I
thought a Christian was—no smoking, no drinking,
be punctual, outwardly a good person, please God
by being good. I tried to run an orderly home.

While we were living this way, the Lord put it in our hearts to go to church. We didn't know anything about different kinds of churches, but our eyes were directed to a little ad in the paper which read something like this, *we don't want you if you're coming to show off your new car, your new dress and to socialize*. In the middle of all the elaborate ads, this one stood out for us. So we went and it just clicked. We knew there was something here that we'd never experienced. It was real.

We weren't born again yet, but we thought we were Christians. Some friends shared with us how easy it was to ask Jesus into your heart and accept Him and let Him do the rest. But I was still searching for God. I decided to get some LSD and find God that way. I dropped the LSD and never have I been so conscious of knowing that drugs were wrong. I knew I blew it. I came on the drug fast and went through a really weird trip. I didn't think I was going to come out of it. I thought I was going to be committed, that I'd really flipped out. I was super embarrassed. Here I couldn't even handle drugs.

The next day two people came along and shared the gospel and we asked Jesus into our hearts. From that moment on we realized the Lord is real and that He has a new life for us. Each day has gotten better and better. The freedom we received just can't be compared with anything that the world has to offer. I was thinking about it today. The peace the Lord gives is like an endless summer vacation. The world is the same, the working and everything. You run into the same problems. In fact, you run into more of them the older you get. But with the peace of God, these other things don't get in the way.

He continues to be patient with me. I murmur when He tries to teach me something. But He leads us on. Being the spiritual head of the house is a challenge. We take our respective positions in the Body that He has ordained for us, even in relation to our children.

I really dreaded having children. I couldn't even love myself or cope with my wife, let alone a child. And it took me a long time—like a couple of months—to get close to Shawn. That is a long time to have a baby every day and not be close. With our second one I was able to understand more about the birth of the child. Well, I talk like I understand! I still don't understand. But I was able to experience the birth of our child and to know the real joy. The Lord really uses our children to show us how we are His children. We really needed two, and the Lord knew it.

I feel the Lord is preparing us for His return. Our home life is being put together and He is showing us the need to reach out to other homes. Our marriage is created anew, our home life is created anew, we have a real love for one another. Right now our ministry is letting people see Him living in us and in our lives. Our relatives knew us the way we were before we met Jesus. They have seen the change in us. Praise the Lord!

The faith and confidence of a life with Jesus is reflected in the lives of those who do accept forgiveness and who go on to live a new life directed by an all-victorious Saviour. "Everyone which seeth the Son, and believeth on him, may have everlasting life" (John 6:40).

Rejoice and be glad

Terry

I came to the Lord before I started with Calvary Chapel. I was sick, in desperate need of blood and I couldn't have blood because of a rare antibody in my blood. I got weaker and weaker and my husband had to hand feed me. I was so sick my father-in-law thought I was dead. In my heart I thought I was going to die.

I can't explain it, but Jesus just came and told me of Himself. I knew it was real. I had a longing and a desire to be with Him. Before He came to me I thought I didn't want to die because of my children. But afterwards I was able to say, "Okay, I know You'll take care of them." And that was so neat. I just praise His name!

Finally the doctors got the blood I needed and built my strength up and I was really looking forward to the surgery. Through it all I knew the Lord was really right there and talking to me. A friend who was a new Christian, came to see me and started talking to me about Jesus. I just lit up and said, "He is real!"

There just happened to be a neighborhood Bible study waiting for me. My husband visited one night when we were studying prophecy. And after that he wanted to visit Calvary Chapel. We started coming and he gave his life to the Lord in a quiet way.

Most recently, I've been learning to really praise

the Lord. It has just been one thing after another at our house, including a lot of sickness. And I tend to praise Him for the things I like! So I just started to praise Him for everything, and there has been a change in me. It is so exciting being a Christian! Really, all the dull days I spent being a non-Christian and searching for material things were a waste. I had everything the world says you need. A husband, three children, a nice home. But I didn't have everything I wanted. My husband used to say, "You know, there is something you really want." He could see it in me. But I couldn't say what it was, because I didn't know.

We have three wonderful children, one is a teenager. The Lord really spoke to me about my kids and told me, "They're mine. Keep your hands off." And I've seen them grow in Him.

As a wife and mother, prayer is one of the most important things I do for my family. My kids are facing things in school and my husband is out working. I'm really pretty sheltered. I can pray for them each day. They need that prayer.

One wonderful thing the Lord has given me is an increased love for my husband. I always loved him, but now I love him so much more. I look at him and say, "I love you so much." Then I don't even see the things that might make me mad at him. That love comes from Christ. And I see it as my ministry to provide a place for my husband to come home to that has this love in it. I think it is a privilege to pray sort of constantly all day and be in fellowship with the Lord. And He just gives me more and more of His love.

Linda and John

John: I moved out here from Pennsylvania. California was buzzing and changing. I thought, "I've been missing out on this all my life!" I tried to catch up but it caught up with me. I got involved in heavy drinking and drugs. I met Linda and we started going to parties together.

Linda: There was a lady where I worked who was a Christian. She started telling me stories out of the Bible. Then I'd see John and tell him the story. I asked her one day how we could accept Jesus. And I kept asking her. I had to get it down pat, exactly step-by-step how we were going to do this. We were reading the New Testament, too. One night we started telling one another the really bad things we'd done to each other during the three years we had gone together.

John: About two days later we knew, this was the time. We got down on our knees by the bed in my bedroom and prayed in unison the sinner's prayer from the Bible in Linda's purse. We were born again at that point but we didn't know it. I guess we spent so much time making the decision, we expected bolts of lightning.

Since then the Lord has brought us closer to Him and our lives have been more abundant. We started going to a Bible study. We got married and went along for about two years, growing in the Lord, going through the dry times, becoming stronger Christians. Then Linda went to the eye doctor because she started having blind spots.

Linda: We'd been praying together about two months before this and I'd had a heavy burden for my mother and my family and relatives. I was weeping and it was really heavy. That night I prayed that God would use me in any way He could even if it meant my life. And I was serious! I'm a chicken really. I don't stick my neck out. I don't know how I prayed that way. When I started having trouble with my eyes, I didn't recall my prayer until John mentioned it.

I went to a neurologist and had tests and then to a hospital for more tests. The doctors found a blockage in my head. By this time I was sure the Lord had me there for a reason. There was someone I was supposed to talk to, and I was ready! I shared Christ with my first roommate who did believe but didn't understand about having a personal relationship. Then my second roommate died before I had shared Christ with her. I had said I was a Christian but we hadn't really talked. It really hit me hard, how precious life is. I kept wishing I had shared the Lord with her. About a week later they told me I needed surgery.

John: There was some kind of a growth which they thought was just outside the vital area of the brain but it was a definite threat to her life. We gave permission to do the surgery, but we told the doctor our trust and faith was in God. The operation went five to six hours, which meant the growth was deeper than originally thought.

Linda's brother and I were playing chess. I couldn't believe the power and the strength the Lord was administering to us. I started praying for Him to give this to the other people, the members of our families. There is a gift of faith God gives to those who ask when it is needed. The heavier circumstances got and the worse the doctors said things looked, the more God's peace came on me. Both sets of parents were accusing me of not being realistic. They said I was running from the facts.

After the operation the doctor said he was sorry he couldn't reach the tumor and that Linda wouldn't live very long, maybe a year. We felt shock and all the natural reactions but the Lord was bearing my burden. You could see the shock on the faces of the family members who didn't know the Lord. It was like all of a sudden they'd caught a steel beam on their back, like the wind had been let out of their sails.

The joy and the peace the Lord was giving Linda and me was blowing our minds, and everyone else's. Linda was in bed with her head shaved and all bandaged from the surgery, just praising the Lord. And her roommate couldn't believe it.

Linda: When they put me in the room, the first thing I did was share about the Lord with the other girl in there. We talked and talked and I was so blessed. I knew the Lord had put me there. One day several people from Mansion Messiah came to see us. They stood at the foot of our beds and sang beautiful songs. I thought I was in heaven and I was crying. My roommate was crying, too. One of the girls in the singing group went over and comforted her. They gave us a picture of Jesus. We put it on the stand between our beds.

Later my cousin came in saying, "Guess what, I just accepted the Lord!" And then she ran out again. I turned around and my roommate said, "Linda, I just accepted the Lord." I was so thrilled!

John: The family didn't want Linda to know what the doctor had said. I kept telling them God was our final hope, the only one we could trust.

Linda: The doctor who gave me the cobalt treatments was surprised because my hair is growing back in the bald spots. He had kind of pacified me, telling me that it might. But he really was hoping I'd just be happy when the other hair grew out long enough to cover the bald spots.

John: Through it all we learned you don't have to be super spiritual for God to do something like this. It is all by faith. And not even an overwhelming faith. While we were praying for Linda to be healed we were praying for our unbelief. We knew we had all the power of the Lord. Linda has outlived her one year sentence and we are planning a trip to Europe. The blockage in her head has retreated enough to allow normal blood flow. We know God will never let us down.

Dean

About six years ago, I was selling Ford cars with a beautiful Christian brother. He witnessed to me and shared Jesus Christ with me until he really provoked me. I was in the world, working with other fellows who thought the same way I did. We had our little off-color stories and we liked to use profanity.

When my mother passed away, this brother Don came over to me and said, "You know, Dean, I really love you." I went home to my wife, Liz, and I said, "Can you imagine a grown-up person like Don telling another grown-up person like me that he loved me?" And I really didn't understand it. But he planted a seed. Then it took three years to start growing.

We moved down to the beach area. Our son David got with some rough characters at the beach and became exposed to drugs. Things got so bad Liz and I didn't know how to cope with it. I went to bed one night so upset that I cried until Liz had to come in and console me. I was just shaking. Finally we both cried out to God to help us. We had gone to church all our lives, but we were really two timers—Easter and Christmas. We thought we were pretty good living people. No one ever told me about Jesus Christ at church. They never asked me if I wanted to be saved.

By the grace of God, the same person who was partly responsible for David getting involved with drugs found the Lord, and he brought David to a Bible study. It wasn't long after that David accepted Christ. Then, of course, it was time to work on the old man.

It was a little while coming. I was kind of stubborn. One night David gave me a hand putting out the trash. It was a beautiful night and Dave just turned around to me and said, "Dad, I think it's time." I knew exactly what he meant. We went into my bedroom and both knelt down beside the bed and there I accepted Jesus Christ as my Lord and Saviour.

I believe God had His hand over Liz and me during the twenty years we did not know Him in our marriage. We have learned that we need to grow together towards Christ. I believe that as we grow in grace, He gives us a stronger love for each other. I really love Liz more now than I did when we were married and it has only been the love of Christ that made that possible. It has brought the whole family together. Christ made the bonds stronger among the three of us and we thank God for the salvation of our family.

I'm so very grateful the Lord found me—I didn't find Him. It just blows my mind to go on Sunday morning and see the converging of these beautiful Christians on that tent. It is really beautiful to be a part of this moving of Jesus. And it is wonderful to know that it is God who is bringing in the people.

Michael

I started taking drugs to find God. The second time I dropped acid, Satan actually came before me as the angel of light and I had such a religious experience that I thought I'd seen God.

I was making $400 to $500 a week as a car salesman. We had incense in the house. I was taking drugs. My wife didn't go for it. We had a $30,000 house, three cars and credit cards—everything middle class America wants and strives for. And I was only 22 years old.

My wife divorced me and I started taking more drugs. And the more I took, the more power Satan wanted to give me. All this time I was still searching for God. I used to go out to the desert and just scream out for Him.

One night I dropped some LSD. Soon as I took it I had a revelation that I didn't ever need to take drugs again. That wasn't where it was at. This was horrible because I knew I had about a 12-hour experience ahead of me. I had just taken acid for about ten days in a row and I was totally removed from reality. Everything was vanishing on me and I knew that I was going to die.

I tried to tell the people I was with that I needed to go to the hospital. They just laughed at me and led me to believe they were going to murder me. And I cried out in my heart to God and I said, "The only reason I've been using drugs is to find You. What a horrible way to die, being murdered."

I felt I was on the outer edge of darkness and all the spirits that I had been worshiping of all the eastern religions appeared to me. They told me, "This is as far as we take you, to death." Then the Lord appeared and they all fled. He said He was the only representative for God and He was pure love. I confessed all my sins and He told me I was forgiven. I stood up and told the people I was with that they could kill me now. I believed Jesus Christ was the son of God and that He had forgiven me for everything. They threw me into a back room and there was an explosion. I thought they had blown the left side of my head off.

I turned myself into a hospital a week later. The original diagnosis was custodial care the rest of my life. At that point I couldn't even feed myself. I spent ten months in psychotherapy just to come to the reality that my fingers were here and my body was here and that I was alive. Then I spent seven months in a group therapy situation learning to interact with people, to know when they were talking to me. But for two years I still thought the whole left side of my head was blown off and I wasn't sure if I was alive or dead.

One night I thought there was an earthquake. The next day nobody had heard about it or felt it and nobody at school knew about it and the papers didn't say anything about it. What did happen was a beautiful presence entered my bedroom. I fell out of bed and said, "God, if I'm having an acid flash or if I'm going to die, take me to heaven." And a still, still voice said, "You have been visited by the spirit of the Lord. If you will follow me, I'll lead you to the people you've always wanted." I had always wanted to be able to express myself to people, to tell them I loved them and to have them love me. I didn't want to hold anything back.

Then I met some of the guys in the music groups who kept inviting me to Calvary Chapel. I said, "Ya, I'll check it out." I checked out Calvary Chapel for a month before I stepped in the doors! On Sundays I'd drive up and down and look at the cars. During the evening services I'd sit in the parking lot and watch all the hippies come. I thought I was being deceived again—longhairs don't go to church. But then when I went in I felt that same love of Christ I had felt the night I overdosed. I said, "God if this is You, I'd like to have some of it." About two or three dozen people came up and told me they loved me and that Jesus loved me. I felt a warmth I'd never felt before.

So I went back the next Friday and they gave an altar call. I was too embarrassed to stand up. But I remembered when I was ten or eleven years old I had accepted Jesus in a little Baptist church in Oregon. And the next words I heard the pastor say were, "Is there anyone here who maybe when he was a little kid accepted Jesus but hasn't been walking with him?" So I figured he really got me! I had finally found the living God.

For the next five to six months I lived in a Christian commune, fellowshiping at Calvary every night, studying the Bible every morning and afternoon, ministering and working in the community.

One night at a prayer meeting I felt I just had to know, am I alive or am I dead. I know I'm saved, but do I have a hole in my head. I had brain damage. The whole left side of my brain wasn't functioning. So I went up and the elders laid hands on me. The Holy Spirit came upon me and I was trembling and shaking. My whole head started glowing. For the first time in two years I had a full normal feeling. As I was crying and praising the Lord, He told me He had given me the spirit of love and power and *a sound mind.*

My wife told me I was nuttier than ever because I was talking about Jesus all the time. She told me I could never see her or my kids again. So I invited her to a hot dog roast down at Corona del Mar beach. Actually it was an ocean baptism for about 2,000 people. We were having a Bible study at the commune when she came in soaking wet from head to toe and smiling from ear to ear. She walked up and said, "Michael, you're not on a trip at all." What had happened was that she went down to the beach and saw the love of Christ and accepted Jesus for herself. I was really rejoicing. The Lord gave me back my wife and daughter and son. My whole family was "remarried" about a year ago.

God raised up a business for me distributing record albums and bumper stickers and tracts. It became a full time ministry and business. My heart is in the ministry and Bible studies. But I learned about business. It started in my garage and built up to five employees. Now I've sold the business and taken over the leadership of Maranatha Music.

I had several thousand dollars in bills to be paid, left over from the time of the divorce. Now with selling the business, I'm in a position to pay off all these people.

In two years of walking with the Lord, I've gone from zero to an abundance. When I left the Christian commune, I had one suitcase. Today the Lord has provided me with a living for my family, a place to live and a ministry for Him. All I can say is that I love Jesus. I continue to praise Him. And I pray that He will keep me in His will daily.

Gloria and Jim

Jim: My mom and sister were Christians and they and all their friends were witnessing to me. Finally, I gave up and accepted the Lord just to please them. Then I moved away from home, got my first apartment and did the things I wanted to do. Satan made it easy for me because I got a job that paid $160 a week. My life was going downhill as I got into a little bit of the dope scene, a lot of drinking, staying at girls' houses. All the time I knew my time was coming, that I was going to have to answer for what I was doing.

I tried Calvary Chapel and I could feel the love. The Bible study was from Revelation and how there would be a time when I could still go to heaven but I'd have to die for Christ's name. So I'm thinking about all this, how I'm a chicken when it comes to pain and dying, about my mom and my friends—all of a sudden my legs were not part of me. They just stood up, I felt the joy of the Lord really come to me.

Gloria: I was living a very sinful life. I was working in an advertising agency. There was a Christian there and every once in a while he would say just

135

exactly what I needed to hear. He would ask me questions that really got me thinking. I knew how unhappy I was. I didn't think anyone else knew, but I had a feeling he knew. All this time I was getting heavier into dope and Satan worship.

Finally, I came to a crossroads. I had to choose. I honestly didn't know which way I wanted. I had no one to turn to except for this one friend at work. I called him and asked him to pray for me. He said, "Where are you! I'll be right there." I told him I was really scared. He talked to another girl at work who was a Christian and she took me to Calvary Chapel. One of the elders there read from the Bible to me. It was dead, no meaning. I wasn't able to understand. I was so desperate, I panicked and thought this is another dead end.

One of the elders said, "Gloria, do you want to accept the Lord?" And I said, "Well, I better go home and think about it and do some more reading." Right then I looked over at the girl who had brought me. She had such a pained look in her eyes and tears were rolling down her cheeks. I thought that was so real, there had to be something behind it. So I said, "Okay, I guess so." I repeated the sinner's prayer and the Lord honored it. I really did feel His joy and peace. My transformation was immediate and complete.

I had really wanted a husband. Along with everything else, I was able to give this up completely to the Lord. One Sunday two weeks later Jim came up and sat down next to me in church. I was attracted to his outgoing personality because I'm not that way. After the service he introduced himself and that was all there was to it. I didn't think too much of it.

Jim: You didn't? I did!

Gloria: Then two weeks later there was a water baptism and both Jim and I were there. When Jim came out of the water, I was the first one to hug him. He hugged me back and then he pulled back and said, "Who are you?" Then he remembered me, and that was it again. But I was kind of thinking about him by now. That next Sunday I walked into church and I prayed. "Lord, you put me where you want me. I feel you want me to talk with someone today. You tell me where to sit."

Jim: I'd been praying about a wife really heavily. But I was praying about another specific girl. As I walked into church I prayed, "Lord, if Gloria is for real, put her right in front of me."

Gloria: I sat down completely oblivious to Jim's presence. And right before the service started I heard this incredulous, "Gloria?" I turned around and I was sitting right in front of Jim. The look on his face I did not understand! Our dates consisted of going to Calvary, prayer meetings and Bible studies. One night we sat on the couch and had a five hour truth session. It seemed like only an hour, but we got everything out in the open. Nothing we have done can be used against us because we have no secrets.

We had a beautiful wedding and our marriage has been the best witness we have for our families and relatives. Within the first eight months we paid off all our debts. We couldn't afford a baby up until that time, but we wanted one badly. When we were ready, we prayed together for a baby and we got Jonathan!

Jim: We decided to go natural child birth and I was with Gloria the whole time. I was really proud of her. Then when the baby came and the doctor said, "He needs some repair work," I just flipped out. The Lord had prepared Gloria by giving her a desire to care for a defective child. But I was unprepared for it. Gloria was ripped up pretty badly in the delivery. We had prepared for a different kind of ending. In this ending I had a son with a cleft palate and a harelip and a seriously sick wife.

Gloria: There have been lots of times I've said, "Why, Lord?" I had a strong desire to have a baby and that was part of the problem. During the time I was pregnant, the baby took first place over Jim and over the Lord. All my life I wanted to care for my own baby. When Jonathan was born I couldn't even do that. It really hurt when my baby was crying and I couldn't go to him. I was bitter.

I said, "Lord, isn't it enough that Jonathan has a defect? How come I have to be damaged, too? I have to have surgery and all this pain." The answer was that it took all of this to put me back into His arms and make me dependent on Him. If I had been all right, I would have spent all my time with the baby and not with the Lord.

I really praise the Lord for everything because He has loved me enough to care about me and not let me slide. I was lukewarm in my love for Him.

Instead of spewing me out of His mouth, He gave me a reheat! It took a long time and a lot of tears for me to see that truth about myself. He really has changed my heart, but nothing short of what has happened would have done the job. It's too bad, but that is the truth.

Jim: We don't know all that the Lord will accomplish in us. I don't think we can understand it all. Jonathan has been used as a witness and I have received a much stronger amount of patience.

Gloria: Just the way we have received all this has been a witness to a lot of people. We love our baby and the Lord is providing physically and financially for him and meeting all our needs. Some people can't believe it!

Jill

In high school I was a song leader and considered popular. From the outside everything was fine, but inside I was crying. Then my mom accepted Christ while I was still in high school. She began praying for her four children and today we all love the Lord.

I began my walk with the Lord five years ago. He has always dealt with me through my own children, using that which was dearest to my heart to tug at me. On one occasion my little girl's fingers began turning green. The doctor said he had never seen a fungus in a child that young. I said, "That's all right. The Lord is going to heal her." And this was even before I had made my real commitment to Him!

My little girl's fingers grew worse and I was broken hearted. About this time the Lord sent a friend who told me about a church where you could go forward to repent at an altar. I was from a much more staid, formal type church. But I went to this church for several months. The week I repented of my sin and really came to the Lord Jesus Christ, He touched my daughter and her fingers began to grow out pink. Within two months you couldn't even tell that there was anything wrong.

From that day forward my life has been a walk

with the Lord and He has become more precious and dear to my heart. Whenever I become a little bit stubborn, I'll see something in my children that troubles me and tell the Lord, "This troubles me." And He replies, "Well, okay, something in you troubles me." I can look at each hard place in a different perspective now. The Bible tells me to count it all joy when I fall into divers temptations, for the testing of my faith worketh patience. "Lord, what's this? I prayed for patience and a trial comes. Your gifts come in strange packages." At each hard place He has accomplished something in me.

When I first became a Christian the Lord began to deal with me on my place as a woman and as a wife. Until I came to the point where He dealt with me in that area, we had a very unhappy marriage situation. I was praying for God to do something with Gary, and what He wanted me to pray was for Him to do something with Jill. He began to deal with me in the areas of submission and of wanting a ministry outside our home. He showed me my place as a wife and mother is in the home. Now the ministry comes, just by person-to-person experiences. Recently the Lord has tucked several new Christians under my wing and He is opening up an opportunity for young women to fellowship in our home.

God showed me I needed working on and when I got in the right place, I wouldn't be a stumbling block to my husband. Then came the growth in my husband's spiritual life. I have a liberty in my life now, a freedom in Jesus Christ. And as I get to know Him more, I love Him more. He gives me a deeper trust.

We see our own weaknesses in our children. Our oldest daughter is the image of me and our youngest daughter is just like my husband. I tend to make excuses for my sins. But if I confess them before the Father I find that deliverance comes from the repentance. And I've almost gotten to the point where when things get rough, I just say, "Thank you, Lord, I know you are doing something through this. Later I know I'll see it."

More and more I see that our children are what we make them. When children are going through rebellious times, many times parents fail to look at themselves. So many parents want something for their children but aren't willing to pay for it. When I get to the point where a situation grieves me, I say, "Okay, Lord. I give You permission to deal with this in me. I know I have no strength in myself to be the person that I should be. That is up to You. But I confess it as sin and I grieve to see it in my children." Then He takes care of it.

I feel so fortunate. My husband is in the world all day. But my job is in the home where I am protected from much of the hectic world. I have quiet time even when I'm doing housework. I am so thankful for what Jesus has done in my life.

Lew

A friend of mine named Kent was heavy into motorcycle riding and drugs. I'd known him for years and years when I saw a miraculous change in his life. He was a completely different person and on fire for Jesus Christ. I asked him what program he was on. He said he had asked Jesus into his heart. I didn't want to do that then, but I went with him to Calvary Chapel.

I had done marijuana and I was into studying my way towards God. The group I studied with said there is no religion higher than truth. I was studying vibrations and energy and light. And whenever I'd see Kent, he'd tell me about the love of Jesus Christ and that I was a sinner. Then I didn't see him for about a year.

I had gone to Calvary Chapel a few times. There was so much love there. I felt I had my finger in a big giant dam and I was afraid that if I took my finger out I'd be flooded with something, I didn't know what. So I got out and went to San Francisco, took more drugs, studied some more. I met a friend and we were both meditating a great deal. I left for three weeks and when I came back his eyes were bright and clean and clear and everything about him was vibrant. And he said Jesus Christ had come into his life and he had a personal relationship with the creator. "Jesus Christ is the way, it is what we've been looking for, Lew," he told me. So I went with him to a church in Oakland and accepted Christ.

I came back to southern California and went back to Calvary Chapel. I really did give my life to the Lord and He lifted my sin and I rejoiced. But then I backslid for almost a year. And again Kent came to me, for the third time. Then I went forward two nights at the Billy Graham crusade because I didn't trust my own heart. I wanted to be sure. I had to ask for faith.

Now I know I am born again and saved. The Lord has blessed me by allowing me to know that I am alive and I am here and I am seeing and the earth turns. Praise the Lord. Living in America, I've known about Jesus since I was a child. Guess I just had to try everything else before I really came to know Jesus.

During the earthquake when all of southern California shook (Feb. 9, 1971), God talked to me. He said, "How solid is your act, Lewie?" I knew my act was built on sand. I had accepted Christ but had backslidden and denied Him too many times. I was playing games. I always really wanted to be a disciple. I thought that would be the greatest thing. As my bed shook, it was like God saying, "Get up, we've got things to do. And that same night there was an eclipse of the moon and that same day *Look* magazine came out with the Jesus Movement on the front cover. That's when things really started happening with me. And my friends came to know the Lord.

I had this idea for a bookstore but I didn't know whether it was the Lord's idea or not. So I just prayed and said, "Lord, you close all the doors if you don't want me to do this." I looked and looked for a place. Finally I found a really nice place that was wrong. When I went to put a deposit on it, I didn't have my checkbook. As I was driving home to get it, my car did a complete right hand turn, zoomed under this building and into the parking lot. I ended up talking with a guy who eventually rented me this space. It didn't happen right away. I wasn't able to get the other place. And this place wasn't even for rent. Here it is—overlooking the Pacific Ocean. It overlooks Sodom and Gomorrah, the sin beaches down here in the summer time. It looks east and west so you can't miss it going up and down the highway. It was just something like what the Lord would do.

I was going to have all the shelving and the desk built for the store. I was up in Costa Mesa to get my logo and a friend saw an ad for a book store going out of business. I zoomed over there as they opened, and here it all is! Just about everything else is donated.

I've been praying for my family. My sister and Mom and stepfather now have come to meet Christ as their personal Saviour. My half brother was backpacking up in Canada and one of the Maranatha groups picked him up and led him to Christ. And another thing I'd prayed for was a Christian girl friend, a girl who was really into the Word. And He gave me that, too.

I've watched the changes in my life, real changes.

How can you describe it—I've got a direction, I've got a purpose, I've got joy in my heart. I rejoice in the hope that I have. I look to the Lord as Saviour and friend, my close friend. I talk to Him continuously. I don't know how He talks to me but all day I hear His voice. Praise the Lord!